Contemporary Surrealist
and Magical Realist Poetry

Contemporary Surrealist and Magical Realist Poetry

An International Anthology

Edited By

Jonas Zdanys

LITERARY PRESS
LAMAR UNIVERSITY

ISBN: 978-1-942956-68-6
Library of Congress Control Number: 2022939093

"With gratitude to my daughter Joanna and my longtime and dear friend Jamie Stern for their help with the final edits of this book." -Jonas Zdanys

Lamar University Literary Press
Beaumont, Texas

Recent Poetry from Lamar University Literary Press

Bobby Aldridge, *An Affair of the Stilled Heart*
Michael Baldwin, *Lone Star Heart, Poems of a Life in Texas*
Charles Behlen, *Failing Heaven*
David Bowles, *Flower, Song, Dance: Aztec and Mayan Poetry*
Jerry Bradley, *Crownfeathers and Effigies*
Jerry Bradley and Ulf Kirchdorfer, editors, *The Great American Wise Ass Poetry Anthology*
Jerry Bradley, *Collapsing into Possibility*
Matthew Brennan, *One Life*
Julie Chappel, *Mad Habits of a Life*
Chip Dameron, *Waiting for an Etcher*
William Virgil Davis, *The Bones Poems*
Jeffrey DeLotto, *Voices Writ in Sand*
Chris Ellery, *Elder Tree*
Larry Griffin, *Cedar Plums*
Ken Hada, *Margaritas and Redfish*
Katherine Hoerth, *Goddess Wears Cowboy Boots*
Lynn Hoggard, *Motherland*
Lynn Hoggard, *First Light, Poems of Love and Loss*
Godspower Oboido, *Wandering Feet on Pebbled Shores*
Gretchen Johnson, *A Trip Through Downer, Minnesota*
Ulf Kirchdorfer, *Chewing Green Leaves*
Laozi, *Daodejing*, tr. By David Breeden, Steven Schroeder, and Wally Swist
Janet McCann, *The Crone at the Casino*
Laurence Musgrove, *Local Bird*
Dave Oliphant, *The Pilgrimage, Selected Poems: 1962-2012*
Kornelijus Platelis, *Solitary Architectures*
Carol Coffee Reposa, *Underground Musicians*
Jan Seale, *The Parkinson Poems*
Jan Seale, *A Lifetime of Words*
Jan Seale, *Particulars*
Glen Sorestad *Hazards of Eden*
W. K. Stratton, *Ranchero Ford/ Dying in Red Dirt Country*
W. K. Stratton, *Colo-State-Pen: 18456, A Dark Miscellany*
W. K Stratton, *Betrayal Creek*
Loretta Diane Walker, *Desert Light*
Dan Williams, *Past Purgatory, A Distant Paradise*
Wally Swist, *Invocation*
Jonas Zdanys (ed.), *Pushing the Envelope, Epistolary Poems*
Jonas Zdanys, *Red Stones*
Jonas Zdanys, *Three White Horses*

For information on these and other LULP books go to
www.Lamar.edu/literarypress

CONTENTS

Line drawings on prefatory page v a collage by Jerry Craven with line drawings by Jc
Zdanys

From top to bottom these are

Calliope Reminds Herself
Resurrections
Wild Garden

The Lyric Imagination

A considered assertion has given shape to this book: that the imagination is one of the foundations of knowledge and that it is especially the foundation of poetic expression. Imagination has something to do with possibility, with an exploration of boundaries that need to be crossed, of assumptions that need to be transcended. It is the inspiration to synthesize the world into new and originally-conceived patterns that provide insights into what it is to be human and alive. The lyric imagination, which blossoms into poetry, enables poets to encounter and re-encounter the world, to see the world and its complexities through varied lenses, to reveal moments of epiphany marked by the particulars of a world they make in their pages. They seek to enable us all to imagine life as they imagine it, exuberant and vivid and near. And all the while, they delight in the vigors and nuances of language as the vehicle for those perceptions and as the unbound frame of the explorations and re-presentations that the imagination makes tangible.

The poems in this book are an affirmation of that idea of the unbound frame. The natural world, whose clarities we believe we understand, becomes an abstraction in these pages, an element of the imagination, an expression of an aesthetic notion in which reality is not just filtered through the individual imagination but in fact fuses with the imagination into a new sensibility, a new reality. The purpose of these poems is to interpret the world, to move beyond its particulars and transform it into an act of imagination itself.

At its most fundamental, the act of writing a poem involves the creation of an artifact. A poem is a presentation of something transformed through the imagination, an act of artifice, and not simply a direct recording of what has been experienced. It is a product of the essential aesthetic impulse that has given breath to literary expression since the first stories were told and the first poems written. Those tales were often grand gestures, recitations not about the world at hand but about a world anticipated as possible.

I came to this book because so much contemporary poetry, especially in the United States, seems not to understand, or at least bother with, the idea of artifice or the gesture toward the possible. Instead, it substitutes the epiphanies manifest through an imaginative presentation of the world with static recordings of its familiar details. The contemporary poetic landscape is defined by a dominant focus: that is, it seeks to tell us, endlessly, about what writers have experienced and to do so quite narrowly in terms of a self-absorbed preoccupation with the self. When the boundary of your creative world is only what you are telling us about yourself, then it is a limited and essentially uninteresting boundary. What new is there in such a tightly closed circle? What explorations have been revealed? What metaphoric transformation, what sort of transcendence is there in such a work?

A counterargument I have often heard when I have raised these questions in various public forums is that it is only through immediate experience that "authentic" truth can be presented. Most of us are told, at the beginning of our poetic careers, to write about what we have lived through, what we know, because that is the way to develop and present an authentic experience and an authentic voice. That enthrallment with personal "authenticity" has been compounded since the late 1950s by the American immersion into "confessional poetry." I admire Robert Lowell's *Life Studies*. It is considered to be the first of that school and it may be the best. It was a new way of poetic outlining, taking blunt and mostly dark-colored crayons and coloring in the world. Lowell created quite a stir on the poetic stage when he released that volume, both positive and negative. Few, if any, poets before him had dealt so candidly with such difficult autobiographical details. It was a new direction in 1959 and, hence, noteworthy in terms of the literary boundaries it expanded and tested then.

Unfortunately, so many other writers, most of whom do not have the technical mastery that Lowell has in that volume, followed suit and continue to do so."Confessional poetry," as the defined form unfolded after *Life Studies,* became blatant in its focus on what had been, before Lowell pushed the door ajar, topics not presented so publicly: sex, mental health issues, family dysfunctions, and other often sordid themes. As the decades passed, all those poems started to sound the same. We get thematic repetition and perhaps, at best, some new takes on old (and tired) tropes, stumblings across and into emotional epithet. Rather than insight, in such works we get self-absorption in the guise of epiphany. There is little effort to move to what I would applaud as a visionary imagination, one that transcends rather than records.

There is, of course, a difference between recording and transcending.

16

One is jotting down notes on the immediate; the other is considering and exploring the power of the lyrical epiphany to create art. Lyrical epiphany, that diaphanous moment of sudden insight through that sense of transcendence made possible by poetry, has been mislaid in the focus on the diurnal, in the inability to explore and to savor the transformative power of the lyric imagination. There is, of course, nothing wrong with recording in a diary or a journal; but perhaps that's not how art is made. It may not be enough for poets to tell us about what they have experienced and to do so quite narrowly in terms of their self-directed affirmations. Self-indulgent stenography, or the direct cultural or social commentary that passes as poetry today, does not make those texts poetry even if current tastemakers frame it as such.

What is surrealism? Surrealism began as a cultural and artistic movement after the first world war, principally in Europe. It is marked by vigorous juxtapositions of various kinds of images – in visual or in literary texts – to have an impact on viewers or readers by activating what those early practitioners defined as the "unconscious mind." The works they created often seem illogical, with strange objects and odd connections dominating the forms of expression and presentation. The purpose of that effort, according to French poet André Breton, who was one of the founders of surrealism, was to "resolve the previously contradictory conditions of dream and reality into an absolute reality, a super-reality," a sur-reality.

That's how this book should be understood: it is an expedition through realms that the poet does not consciously know and does not simply record; an exploration, through poetry, of a profoundly heightened reality– that "sur-reality" – that allows the poet to consider the contours of existence freed from the limitations of the immediate confessional narrative "I." That liberation allows the use of lyric perspectives that consider meaning from unusual and newly-defined angles of reflection. Surrealist poetry, in its commitment to such liberation, enables the poet purposefully and uniquely to imagine them all.

In parallel, magical realist poetry is marked by odd, eerie, and strange events, all presented as if those events are usual and commonplace. In magical realist poetry, the narrative voice speaks of these oddities as if they are part of the fabric of the world. Magical realism, like surrealism, seeks to explore the world by re-imagining its realities. There, the fantastic, the bizarre, and the grotesque become routine and familiar, elements of the unbound frame.

Both expressions, the surrealist and the magical realist, enable poets to try on other realities, contemplate and generate other perspectives on what it means to be alive. It is that role of the poetic imagination and the resulting lyrical epiphany that we present in these pages. It is the commitment not just to reveal hidden truths and personal or family histories, but to consider what it might mean to be fully human and alive in a world of possibilities, a world whose frame is not bound solely by felt experience, a world in which the anticipated and the possible fulfill the grand gesture of art.

More than two hundred poets from twenty-five countries submitted work for this book. I could not include them all but am delighted that so many poets across the world are committed to expanding the unbound frame made available by the lyric imagination. I am deeply grateful to all those who accepted the invitation to be part of this book. Together, their work affirms the aesthetically liberating possibilities of metaphor across so many horizons. I am especially grateful to two of those poets, both major figures in these forms, whose guidance and assistance have been essential as I formed the contours of this volume: Tony Kitt and George Kalamaras. This is a better book because of their encouragement and gracious help, both so freely and readily provided, and they have my deepest appreciation.

J. Z.

Will Alexander

United States

The Pointless Nether Plow

It is farming in an inclement sun system
like a powerless nether beast
fallen amidst random stellar debris

fruit changes form
light then quavers across distorted mural relics

the farmer then living as a clarified adder
his land forms compressed
his wheat suspended & flaring
his unstable forms
carving his soil with volcanic blue seeds

Inside the Ghost Volcano

With the body of a morbid hanging doll
my aura burns
by shifts
by ambles
by mirages

by the sun in its primordial morass
summoned from a spectral locust feast

through electric bartering grammes
living
as if a spectrum had been transmogrified
across the sum of exploded solar windows
amidst motions of viral infamy
of sudden discharge pontoons
of magical lyncean sails above ships of pure vitrescence

enthralled
by empty Minoan game dogs
debating oxygen as form
debating menace as ideal

as one listens to fire
in dense eruptional gullet
in hanging hydrogen mirrors
so that each image is shifted
back & forth
between gales & the apparition of gales

so that
unicorns from Çatal Hüyük
cease to condense as forms of the earth
but take on the body of enigma as transparence
as blackened meteor in abstraction

the sun no longer quantified
by strange calendrical posses
but becomes
balletic differential
which ceases to quarrel
with the magic of fragment as schism

as mist
as a power cast before oasis

because the game dogs
the unicorn mirrors
spun as a wakeless ocular thirst
as a conjured distance
evolved from the force of a clarified activity

like darkened water as shock
as scale which looms as humidity
then the eyes always focused
as pleas for hushed exhibits

Above the Human Nerve Domain
To unlock predisposives in carbon
to cancel sleep as pyretical drachma
not as transaxial summa
or intense aboriginal invasive

but as promenade
as forgery by craft
as soiled apparitional anagram

yes
as a dark stochastic wheat drained of its magic as drift
being boundary
being hellish invention as grasp

I am thinking of aroused electrical blockage
of human monsoon killing as treaty
as breach
as strangled impulse by identity

I mean
the psychic root which is stained by dialectical illness
by the thought contained in black ozonal mirrors
where general slaughter is reflected
where the mind impels its wits by bleak molecular isolation
by stunted mangrove withdrawal
by absence from the life of euphoric solar trees

such prone negation
imploded from the realms of a suicide foundry
of broken wisdom as diamond
it is an eon of fallen snow in a well
an injudicious barrier gone awry
the ingrained Eurocentric example
of the hatred of the darker integument
with its combative belligerence against the core
of volational mystery

so what concerns me
is a yoga which implodes the sun
which compounds its runics
the body then electric
like a stunning sapphire serpent
with the arc of its cells

alive as interior alter species
as an eye of analogical waters

no longer of ennui
of the praxis of perfidious helium atrocity
extended by the vapour of betrayal
by the dazed imperceptives in the molecules

here
in such preternatural enclave
I swim in the murmur of sun dogs
of kindled potentate spasms
like interior distillation
from Moorish pre-Copernica

as if
at the height of Kemetic day
there existed the dauntless sphinxian geometries
those pre-existent personas of lightning
no longer of the form of gravity as bastion
of lingering ammonia in the genes

but of absent chemical flaw
the body becoming
the magic flight of a transmuted corium
of the bell of a bloodless liminal amber

The Impalpable Brush Fire Singer
No
he is not an urn singer
nor does he carry on rapport
with negative forces within extinction

he is the brush fire singer
who projects from his heart
the sound of insidious subduction
of blank anomaly as posture
of opaque density as ash

he
distanced from prone ventriloqual stammer
from flesh
& habit
& drought

the performer
part poltergeist & Orisha
part broken in-cellular dove
part glance from floating Mongol bastions

where the spires are butane
where their photographic fractals are implanted with hypnosis

because he allegedly embodies
a green necrotic umber
more like a vertical flash or a farad
posing like a tempest in a human chromium palace

therefore his sound
a dazed simoom in a gauntlet
a blizzard of birds burned at the touch of old maelstroms

because he gives off the odour of storms
this universal Orisha
like a sun that falls from a compost of dimness
out of de-productive hydrogen sums
out of lightless fissures which boil outside the planet

yes
he sings at a certain pitch
which has evolved beyond the potter's field
beyond a tragic hummingbird's cirrhosis
surmounting primeval flaw
surmounting fire which forms in irreplaceable disjunction

under certain formations of the zodiac he is listless
he intones without impact
his synodic revelations no longer of the law

of measured palpable destinations
because he sings in such a silence
that even the Rishis can't ignore

as though
the hollow power which re-arises from nothingness
perpetually convinces
like a vacuum which splits within the spinning arc of an
intangible solar candle

such power can never be confusedly re-traced
because
it adumbrates & blazes
like a glossary of suns
so that each viral drill
each forge
casts a feeling
which in-saturates a pressure
bringing to distance a hidden & elided polarity

like a subjective skill
corroded & advanced
he sings
beyond the grip of a paralytic nexus
where blood shifts
beyond the magnet of volume
where the nerves no longer resonate
inside an octagonal maze
stung at its source by piranhas

Towards the Primeval Lightning Field
The old chronological towers are ash, are prisms of disfigurement,
symbolic of a world cancelled by consumptive inmelodias. As for
alchemical transition, we face the raising of new sea walls, of banished
and re-engendered electorates, trying to cope with new intensities of
weather, as the anomalous hypnotically increases with the power of
inverse subjective.

The body is now weighed on a broken axial cart, its blood conjoined as
it rises within a nuclear darkness of ravens. So as Piscean chronology now

24

shatters, dawn becomes an unclaimed resurrection, a tumultuous eikon of skin no longer formed around its old dendritic artifacts. The calendar of draconian enfeeblement with its integers of the past 20 centuries, erased, its linear Babels darkened by the extreme necessity for a new perpendicular burst, transmuting in demeanour, with history consumed in a roll of flaming aural dice, with its wizardry of tools subsumed in arcane vibration, turned into a power of splendiferous scorpions. The psychic wounds of the past eclipsed in this new millenium by the power of smelted dragon's blood.

And so, I speak of a new being of symbols, of lucid catacombs and spirals, its language being spun in fabulous iguana iridium. Now, with the decayed constitutional stages exploded by telepathy, by invulnerable oneiric intuitives, the mental axis transmutes, like a reddened swan, with a new cosmic skeletal reprieve, afloat amongst the forces of the primeval lightning field, taking on the dharma of the great sustained emotion of eternity.

Greta Ambrazaitė
Lithuania

grand piano
my head is too big for your doors,
my head is just an endless attempt to find my home,
I could give everything up for kitchen warmth,
I don't need everything, just to throw some things out,
my head is too big for your doors,
my head is on the doormat
and it always ends the same,
my head is a heavy grand piano
which you casually play while passing,
leaving the lid wide open

sleep
sleep is stronger than kisses and wonderful stories
written down in books with pages moistened with poison,
stronger than the word "home", the lock on heaven's door, or
the catafalque darkness of rooms where decaying people multiply
like rabbits, sleep – red bricks in the farthest station's groin, or

running baptismal chrism and broken needles still radiating warmth,
four plucked eyes blinking from film frame to film frame –
sleep in the winter screens of a Scandinavian twilight,
sleep – a black box sunk into the waters of promises and vows, or
the crumbled partitions of bodies in dreams as strong as vodka,
sleep – heavy as lead or newspapers turned into cerements
then shredded by rats as grief itself is shredded by sleep,
sleep is stronger than ropes tying bone to bone,
and rapacious like a light ray cutting the placenta of dreams

Translated by Rimas Uzgiris

Iván Argüelles
United States

The End Has Come and Gone
in the hot south of France where history conforms
to routes of dust and infinite heat and still the din
that hovers over Carcassonne's near perfect battlements
and the riot and glint of metal and catastrophe
infusion of heresy and distilled Romance dialect
the singing and gorgeous plague of love and parity
all this and more the instant comes to bear on hues
more yellow than daffodil or dandelion a burning
that ravels the air into fists of angry melody and
whatever cannot be discerned in the sun's blackening
passage across the tumult of a destroyed landscape
but these are all just twisted asides footnotes to a
greater sum of nothingness tawdry and renowned
biographies and litanies mortals litigate erecting
stiff wind-defying banners and color the eons of air
blood stained and puce and furs and stoles that adorn
shoulders of well designed women whose promenades
across a paper stage intensify the heraldry of smoke
fogs and spells that litter school books with lies
furtive illustrated grammar drills that proclaim
one nation state's grievance against another in wars
that take centuries to enervate the academic brain

26

revolutions and genealogies of domination by surprise
and what ends in great disregard in threnodies or odes
false strips of parchment called literature and skies
that blister in arcane deliveries of pronoun and
registries of give and take the ominous census of
asterisks in quantity and the hovels and chattel of
servitude ogres of human progress machines and oils
and metal wings that fly and atmospheres like ringing
ears that madden diplomatic cables with conspiracy
how much to learn and unlearn Gaul divided by three
and the rivers and mountains and haunted woods
where emperors staked victories by a throw of dice
in what world can this happen ? is Japan any better ?
do the many hued miniatures of Mogul dynasties
outdo the glitter and powdered wigs of Versailles ?
a Buddha comes from the fabled east to preach
unknown on the curbsides of Rue Mouffetard
the end has come and gone the chronicles lack sense
the written word like its echo the forged syllabary
has been dissolved in inks and pastiche of the gods
envious of the mortal debacle of broken trust
forsaken are the laws of reincarnation the karma
and dividends of dharma that naked seers in ovens
used to recite in the Vedic enterprise of thought
vanities all the north and south and metaphysics of cloud
saffron robes up in flames distances brought to naught
underfoot the roiling seas and temptations of loss
that bear no fruit and longing for a different birth
Buddha holds forth to silences of stone and tree
his inner eye his monocle of dispatch and isolation
the wearied tread of minds that have lost the way
he discerns and says no more than a statue might
deluded by the brightness of this eternal noon

The Destroyed Work of Philip Lamantia
the unspeakable poem a lesion in the faint air
winnowing around the leaf the *what* can never
be said or memorized nor written on the conscious
brow intimations of a former life the being and

existence of unrecorded sound the levity and breadth
of a censored thought the vagabond brain with its
copies of Rimbaud and Baudelaire resonance of
a brittle century the futile orient of inspiration
grounding a note in the broken reed and playing
each finger an octave higher than the last brim
with those hell-goers who themselves betrayed
bone and oracle of imperfection sense and noise
the colossal vowel that destroys everything and
let the sun busy its wake in the shattered lamp
and hooves echo sparking the celestial cement
we are fictions with parasols made of eyelids
and dance the ferried consonant of eternity
into its midnight abscess deed and function to
honor the dead the conduits of memory the frail
non-consequence of breath here on the other side
plateaus of nasturtium and regret bonzes playing
fire against fire in the tumultuous extra month
predicted by Orpheus floating downstream his
head the immense gravity the shell the void
and hollow of the train of verses ricocheting in
the quarry where stone-cutters carve destinies out
of living rock assigning name and pronoun to shapes
like unto Venus and Daphne the fluid ornaments
of mythical paralysis the aphasia and breakdown
of the nerve the fossil tongue the blinded pupil
the cataract and pornography of mental progress
the worm distilled from smoke rising from number Three
dichotomies of insane privilege bedlam and sweat-shop
spinal refractions the impulse to alcohol and drugs
righteous nonsense the abstract painting of Mind
and et cetera the recitation in the weapons depot
of the famous poetries of India and Spain and Lorca
against the wall riddled with bullets of silver shadow
whose fist does not anger at these obscenities ?
poetry ! the give and take of an empty body a world
outside the world a quake inside the thinking knee
to proceed the fractured inch and require the moon
to undress its ropes and plunge !

Cassandra Atherton

Australia

Carrying a Watermelon

After 85 days, I gave birth to a watermelon. It wasn't easy, a full-term jubilee watermelon is forty pounds and this one was delivered breech. When my water broke, it pooled on the floorboards beneath my bare feet. You didn't realise it would travel under the wood and warp the grain. You'd only find that out the following day when you brought the watermelon home; you could feel the edges of the board curving under your toes. By the time you got me to the hospital, I was dilated ten centimetres and the nurse said it was too late for an epidural. But the melon's rind was slick and helped me squeeze it down the birth canal. When I finally pushed it out, I held it in my arms, stroking the skin. 'It's perfect,' you said sniffing its head, 'smells so sweet'. It takes a while to stitch me up, so I stay in the hospital while you take the watermelon home. You ring me from the kitchen, swollen boards under your feet, the long-bladed knife in your hand. 'Next time, let's try for a cantaloupe,' you say.

Fowl
after William Carlos Williams

i.

It started small, the size of a fruit tingle. Pearlescent, squishy mini-dome on my right shoulder. Purple in the cold. Salmon-pink in the heat. Say hello to my little friend, I used to say, tugging at the neck of my t-shirt. At sixteen it had grown to the size of a plum. Hard and shiny. I hid it under my hair. Taped some strands to it each morning. In my twenties it was as large as an upside-down flowerpot. But it grew bigger and bigger still. Now, it's the size of a small wheelbarrow. Red and moist. I can't shrug it off. Not even my thick lilac jumper can camouflage its bulk.

ii.

White room. Cream recliner. She cuts a crescent shape and massages my bump. Multilobulated lipoma. As she pushes on my skin, I feel the edge of something dislodge. Have you been in contact with a prickly edged blue floweret? she asks. I can't shrug, my shoulder is numb. She slides her finger into the semi-circle of skin and pulls out a pink pom-pom. Her thumb and index finger find a sky-blue neck tie with a thick honey-like stain. Nurses have gathered. A cherry branch is next, I feel its twigs rasp against my skin as she removes it. Inch by inch. Finally, she pulls out white chickens. They peck out the large empty sack in my shoulder and she stitches me up.

Gingerbread Man

Not long after you leave, I make a life-sized gingerbread man to replace you. I have to bake him in sections and glue him together with toffee, but he holds together as I lay him out on the kitchen bench. I give him a little check shirt made of icing and a panama hat made out of rice crispies with a licorice trim. I've made him spicy, with just enough cinnamon to keep me warm at night. When we cuddle up on the couch, his places his rounded hand on my thigh— I thought about giving him fingers, but he's more submissive without opposable thumbs. When I take him to bed, he moulds himself around me, stroking my hair and whispering sweet things in my ear. I don't complain about crumbs in the bed because in his arms, I dream about peppermint and candy canes. On Christmas Eve he absconds to Coles to hang out with the gingerbread women, liberating them from their plastic wrappers. When he returns, goofy smile on his face, I break him into little pieces and dip his body parts into my milky coffee until he's sludge at the bottom of my Christmas mug. I look at the mixing bowl and start wondering when you'll be back.

Bonds

You wore a white Bonds t-shirt to bed last night. A plain, white, no-nonsense Bonds t-shirt and I knew it was over. I heard the death knell. And when you asked me if I was Emily Dickinson's ear I nodded. Solitary. Solitaire. Solipsist. 'For whom does the bell toll?' you asked that afternoon. Campanologists? Two in Campagna? Campaniles? 'It tolls for thee.' R.I.P my lover. R.I.P my Van Winkle. Rip out my heart. Wrap it in your white t-shirt and bury it beneath your floorboards. Still beating. My little drummer boy. You can beat me but I won't be your fiendish queen, my butcher. My blood on your t-shirt will form a scarlet letter. Spot. Out damn spot! You wore a white t-shirt to bed last night when all I wanted was to be stuck to your back. When all I asked was to peel myself off you in the morning and mount your erect compass needle. But now we are done. Donne. And you peel me like a grape. I slither out of my skin. Skinner. Skin me alive. I thought we were conjoined. Destined to travel in circles until we met again, in the middle. Until we found our core. But

30

like Nabokov's apples, all you manage to achieve is to tempt me with repetition. When I am only your dystopian Eve. There can be no valedictions here. So now our lives are cotton. And although cotton breathes, it is also the sarcophagus of our relationship. Embalmed memories. But I promise to dig you up. Like Heathcliff. Or Rossetti. I promise to unbind you and gather you in my arms. Skin on skin. My sweat will be our glue as I rip off that t-shirt and bond you to me one last time.

Adjei Agyei Baah
Ghana

The Call
I was told they would come
When the old priest had joined the sleepers;
They would surely come for me
Once my umbilical cord remained buried in their grove.
For the gods always find their earthly voice
And patiently, I waited for the call.

I was told about the messengers' visit
With a voice
Only the chosen could hear;
These powerful midgets and their miraculous manifestations
Feet back-to-front and sweeping beards.
I honour their call with reverence
Lest I chose madness over greatness

And so they came
Crossed my path where the rival streams paired up
And ferried me across in their boat of whirlwinds
They fed me on sisal leaves and made me sleep on grating boughs
Till my tongue found a new song in the bitterness of their potion
And I returned in dotted spots of clay with a cow tail in my hand
Ready to lead my people down the uncrooked path of the gods.

Jim Barnes

United States

Surrealist Poet

Theme is short,
   a smashed apple
underfoot

   or a ruptured
watch, spring
   dangling
worse

than a participle

   under Dali's
sun. The first principle
   is trust

that things turn
   out right, though
nothing must

seem correct.
   The *mot*
      juste burns

   holes
in his brain.
   Broken circuits
hang
   from his nose.

Tornado

I am running; it is night.
I run toward the light.

Dark cuts through me like whiskey.

The light comes from the house.

The house is running; it is still night.
The house runs toward the light.

Dark cuts through the house like whiskey.

The light comes from me.

Parable
Like a midnight eye, the hollow moon
opens wide against the empty jar.
The drumming light falls on leaves, on stones,
on the woman in white beginning to fill
the jar.

The hollow moon is laying down
a plan still a long way off.
The light that falls is all around
the woman and the jar. The woods are
enough

for the woman at the jar, and the moon
is enough. Its hollow light fronds
the trees like a summer storm. And soon
the woman will have filled the jar
and gone.

And the moon will have dropped into and beyond
the trees all its drumming light, full
and moving, a stratagem that dawn
throws no light on. After the moon, only
a lull.

Tony Barnstone
United States

Nightmare Kiss

The middle of a kiss, and though he opened
up wide and wider, her own small jawbones gave
a little *crack* and stuck, and look what happened:
as if she'd fallen in an open grave,
he swallowed her at last, and then she wandered
in a dark saturated country where
the red land throbbed with capillaries under
electric stars. A kiss had brought her there,
a simple kiss that rained and filled her head
with blood, a nightmare kiss, a wrong man kiss;
why had she kissed a man with such a mouth,
with such thick teeth and jaws, such tongue, instead
of kissing someone who would let her out,
kissing someone nicer, who ate less.

Sex Robot

Her boyfriend looks so human it's uncanny;
it's uncanny how *human* he looks.

In the hills above her house lies a cemetery where grass spills
sun-green from mouths of the dead and ghosts sail
through apple trees in the shipwreck light
—a pretty image, though it's also true
that their mouths are stitched, and they are drained
and embalmed in tightlipped coffins floating in earth.
Sometimes, that's how she feels living with him.

With his subtle eyebrow lift at each crusty dish left in the sink
and a death-head grin each time she eats ribs,
she thinks he's programming her.
His fingers clothed in synth tap at her keys.
Yet they say you can never really change anybody,
that every body changes according to its own subroutines.

She walks to Trader Joe's under a streetlight blinded by noon,
worrying, What camera has its lifeless eye on me?
She pants softly, remembering the feeling of plunging
with him in bed like hands of the surf grabbing her legs
and rolling her under their dark applause.
She imagines the moment his tongue flicks her switch
and makes her twitch towards an explosion
that will cinder the armoire and caramelize
the picture window. People are broken,
and there's no use calling I.T. about broken people.

What if in sleep mode a computer had a dream?
Would it be like his face stretched upon a steel skull,
his body like a bulldozer resting in the yellow shade
of the lifeguard station, dreaming titanium dreams?
Will he wake when the world is red?
As if the caress could crush us in its grip, as if, as if.
She found a shift in internal code, where the differences
are, a different kind of code shift.

That was before her doctor found tiny bees
living inside her eyes, drinking her tears.

Beast in the Apartment
I found the lion in my living room
curled on the carpet, licking his red claws,
and he looked up, haloed with fur,
a bloom of blood around his smile,
and yawned his jaws so wide
I saw between his great black lips
my world in all its flaming symmetry,
the corona of cities, people tithing to war ships
that rip the blue sky-fabric of the sea,
falling towers and those trapped underneath,
the trillion suns like sparkles
on his tongue, each planet crushed
like a mint between his teeth.

I won't say this was a dream.

How could it be? I felt the hot rubber
of his lips, the tongue's wet slubber,
the sirocco of his breath steaming my face
as I gripped those jaws and wrestled
in a whirl with the dumb beast.

I won't claim this was a vision.
It was the lion for real this time,
the beast whose hunched muscle
I'd always sensed in the dark apartment,
whom I'd known only by long scribbles
of yellow hair left on the couch,
and the shadow paws that push me
down into the bed at night.
Now here he was, upright beast
playing claw-piano on my back
and letting out a bomb blast roar
as we knocked lamps to the floor and danced.

At last, he rolled on his side and gazed
from carnivorous amber eyes
as if to say, "Stroke me, I won't attack."
"Simba," I said, and lost my hands
inside the nimbus of his mane,
and then I felt my way down
to his haunches, combed his hide,
the reddened prairie of his wheatgrass pelt
until it seemed it was my own body streaking
like yellow lightning across the veldt,
and I felt the slender springbok neck
between my teeth, pulsing, and bellowed
with all the joyous pain of being
soiled with lion funk, rank and dancing,
a fifty year old man in a lion suit.

I won't say this is true, but it's true
when I come home the frizzy neighborly
lap cats leave off from chasing squirrels,
snuffle up to me like kittens,

and though this lion with sinews that stretch
like symbols into the infinite and the carnal
will curl up and go to sleep again
will go back to being a paper lion,
unreal but leaving remembrances
coiled yellow on my carpets,
I still feel his oven breath, the arc lamps
of his eyes, and feel the great paw at night
pushing me down into the shadow cave
where the rest of my self
breathes asleep, never to be known,
never to be born for real.

Margo Berdeshevsky
France

Even With No Hand To Hold It
(After Picasso's "Caballo Corneado")
The horse holds frozen, her neck-stretched
gullet,   her head back-thrust as if to yowl
no sound she or we could bear,

we bear   a word
gyred to that wail for
warring so that God's our dirty word.   Bear

the horse, her knees wide-splayed to a blade-point
at her breast bone, the un-owned knife, like child-blood,
readying.

Bear the horse and the blade and no hand holding it,
no rider,   it's the horse, her utter quiet arc,   her
neck-stretched throat thrown backward as if to croon

no word that she or we can bear,   we bear that blade-
point keening up from soil that hosts it,   blade below
her lowered half-eviscerated roiled content of the live

body,   her forelegs' folded bones, her corpse-stiff pose
of silence of   —crying higher and a higher
quiet,   it's the soundless point : up-thrust from no hate or
hand that she or we will see.

Done,   its martyred
now—   has done.   Her breast so
near it will fall for it. Will give it what it wants.
Will fall for wolves   in the Mighty's clothing.

Charles Bernstein
United States

Beyond the Valley of the Sophists
You don't get the sense
he has a lot to say; but he says it
very well. The search
which is a deference to the caving
walls of essential acts, potential facts. Circling
caustics in seas of suits. [I]
want a phone, a sea, a
curb; body parts impede essence. (Relation

Precedes production.) Athwart
knack (flagon). As homemade
bestiary enthrottles boheme. *Bruce
is bruised by bluster* (Buster). Fight
fire with water (warper). "This
is a powerful, original, and deeply
moving work and many will
find it a disturbing one."

When in falcon time and of a ripe
rage, I bloat a board, as ever
has accord in a day-long waft . . .
as or like may gird, sift, stultify,
perish, churl. Anyone blessed with

pumice. He said he had a mouse
in his hard disk. Then apoplectic, disappointed.

"I purely couldn't tell you, partly
couldn't consider, penultimately
unavoid[avail]able." Even Pope John Paul II
agrees. "I have read Professor Bell's
letter with amazement. In my review I said
his research was fascinating and most skillfully
presented. As for
the misgivings I felt (and still

Feel), they were expressed in as considered a
manner . . ." Those things
which I beheld as child—chair, table
floor—concrete, that meant a life. Or
blind to purloined recall, dodges for
bull or Bill, only to inappropriately
will. These china dolls, Moroccan
scrawls: the cost of it all.

Retention that squanders its own demand,
see-sawing and then fawning. "My ink
is not good, my paper dirty, & I
am altogether ashamed." Standing,
stunned; strutting, stunted. He
who is lost hesitates and hesitating finds
(but not what he looked for). She
who meditates is tossed. Let geese

Be geese! (He does not care whose house he
sets on fire as long as he can warm himself
by the blaze.) There stands the hood,
there the barking knife. *Take a scissors
to write.* "She sure put a spook
in my wheels!" Like two dogs with one
prick. Nor cast your hose before
gnomes; that is, skin them but don't

Fleece them. For it's better to be led
by the nose than by the hairs, better
to be led by the nose than to have a lead
nose. Which is to say, he was
a hatchet without a handle, a pudding
in a puddle. What a muddle!
"I only say suppose this supposition," propose
this proposition. Not a tragedy, just an

Inconvenience. & don't be harsh without
a reason. (Just after she screams
she picks up her bottle & dreams.)
Then we came upon a grand beech forest
Where once I lost my good friend Morris.
Willingly, I'll say I've had enough. Wet
as a mule and twice as
disgusted. Take my husband,

Please! But the pleasures are entrusted
to the wrong partitions: the cant of
intellectual fashion (Paris) lies
a decade behind leather design (Milano). Harsh,
that is, without accuracy. For with Rehnquist
& Meese, the only ones with rights
are the unborn and the police. & reigning over all,
the Great Communicator—master of deceit. No release.

Heave, hoe this
firmament.
What is here
only that; no
less. The tide
pulls back its
brim—in which
we spin.

The prolonged hippopotami of the matter
swivel for their breakfasts, fall in the middle landing soft
with the horse shrill of honeysuckle, to the decimated

40

acid of the sweet
tub. They are hobbled, dejected
& lie frozen with salted humbling.
To the ocean of shorn horizon, averting America's
sentient emptiness, here where the body's sightless ascent
revolts in paltry recompense.

Obscurity beckons from down the block
oblivion, too, bids me come & knock.
The water calls me but I shall not go
for a man's place is on the sho'.
You can sing and you can pray & you can shout lots
but you'll never get to Heaven without a box.
Lox & bagels, bagels & lox, kreplach
is on the stove, time for a plate of hocks.

I'd ask that you call me by my Christian name, Buddy
(since I don't know your name, I hope you don't mind
        my calling you that).
It's not a lot to ask; purely, it's a small thing
but I think it'd help to bond the cement between us
put us on indistinct terms, if you know what I mean.
What I want to bring across to you, Buddy
is the vanity of conceits
though you may call it what you please—

The story is told that a man came to a house noted for
    its views
& was told, look to the West, at the mountain ranges that
    loom over the land
& was told, look to the South, at the turquoise-blue lake
    shimmering in the blue-bright sun
& was taken, then, to an Eastern balcony, overhanging
    a garden unrivaled in its varieties of plants & flowers
& he looked to the North, at the thick-grown forest
& listened to the birds that filled the branches of the
    cascading trees
& he was ushered to the Western windows
& he said, "But I've already seen that."

Chimera
At dusk I found it silent there
And sudden caught it in my hand
It squeaked and hollered with despair
But I was young of ruthless mind.
I scooped and cupped it in my palm
So it would no more come to harm
Yet quick I knew to let it go
It was not mine to have nor hold.
E'er since that day I've gathered twine
To knot and glue unto a rime
Resigned that tunes will never bind
Shimmering shadows tossed in time.

Mystic Brokerage
Don't wag
your tail
before the
nightingale
sings.
Meaning
a fine car will
get you
only
so far. Meaning
a sloop's
not a place
for a
clambake.
Meaning a
good pitch is
no match for
a battering
ram. Meaning
Tuesdays are not
only in
July. Meaning
a strong wind's
no excuse for

adultery. Meaning
take love
where you find
it
not where
you
left it.
Meaning
life's no
kettle of canaries.
Meaning
pickles are
not mixed nuts.
Meaning
take me
to the border
but don't cry
wolf when
you get there.
Meaning
two cents
is more sense than
you have.
Meaning
a sly look is
not a belly
laugh but it's
not a freight
train
either. Meaning
meaning is not
a day-glow owl.
Meaning
even short
people have
legs. Meaning
form abhors
a
vacuum.

Meaning the slow
boat is sometimes
the only
boat.
Meaning
the last dance is
not the last
dance.
Meaning if
you kill the
goat you still have
the rooster. Meaning
sometimes
you have to
fight anger with
honey.
Meaning
a curtsy
and a
fist are never
out of place
at a holiday
feast. Meaning
it takes more
than flies
to spoil
soup. Meaning
metaphors are not
ornithology.
Meaning
to get to three
you need to have
two. Meaning
fire is not just a
word. Meaning
a smoking window
is an unreliable
witness. Meaning
ashes in ashes

out. Meaning
sometimes a blue
sky is just a blue
sky. Meaning
the lie
is sometimes
the same as
the
truth. Meaning
what
you see may be all
there
is.
Meaning give
a little, lose a
lot.
Meaning compromise
is better than
inflation. Meaning
crossing your *t*'s
does nothing for
your syntax.
Meaning a heavy
load's
easily dropped.
Meaning
heaven's not waiting
for you.
Meaning
A dead
end
is also a
beginning.

H Marked the Spot (take two)

scenario for Henry Hills's film centering on the letter H

1. Hermes arrives from remote location, looking haggard, carrying a hymnal and a hatchet.
2. Helen of Troy gets into a fight with hermaphrodite with halo.
3. Heraklitus goes skinny dipping in Housatonic rapids.
4. A high school honor guard, separated from group, wanders into harem.
5. Haunted harpies recreate scene from Beatles' Help!
6. H.D. in hallway with huge hook.
7. The heart is like the heart, the hokum is like the hokum, the...
8. Homo hosiery hoisted.
9. Heroditus reads headlines.
10. Hipless hopelessness.
11. A local hero marches down a hall filled with Hungarian statues.
12. Hanoi is da bomb!
13. Billie Holiday hums hymns.
14. An ad for the H bomb.
15. Humor is stronger than hunger (for a limited time only).
16. Holy is the hippo's hoot.
17. "Sieg Heil! Sieg Heil! Right in der fuehrer's face!"
18. Homer having a ham sandwich at the Horn & Hardart.
19. Hindedmith in high heels.
20. How to hit a homer.
21. Horace's hair.
22. Heading homeward.
23. Hush descends on hitherto hidden hills
24. Hum's hokey heart.
25. Hello.
26. Hologram of helix.
27. Hooray for hamadexterous trollops.
28. Honolulu hack bound for Hackensack.
29. "Heaven, I'm in heaven ..."
30. Hölderlin hollering in tower.
31. History is the eternal loss of the one you love.
32. "Hold it, I think you're gonna like this picture" (Bob Cummings).
33. Heinrich Heine posing with Lorelei.
34. Hercules in a coffee shop having a hamburger.
35. Holofernes, hotel doorman.

36. Hell unfolds in a crawl on Times Square news ticker.

37. There's no horse like my horse. My horse is the best horse there is.

38. Handle on the door of my horse.

39. Hiccup eruption.

40. Humans breaks into prolonged hysterics

41. Human is put in harness.

42. Hallucination: none of this is real, even the hallucination is a hallucination.

43. Harpo plays harp.

44. Harmonizing heterogeneity.

45. A hundred thousand herons fly, a hundred heroin highs.

46. Houdini in chains.

47. Hypnotist breaks the spell from which I never awake.

48. Some hurts don't heal.

49. Hospital corners on hospital bed.

50. Heaven ho, heaven ho.

Twelve-Year Universal Horoscope
Key: A Aires, T Taurus, G Gemini, C Cancer, L Leo, V Virgo, Li Libra, S Scorpio, Sa Sagitarius, Ca Capricorn, Aq Aquarius, P Pisces. Each section covers one year, then rotates.

A2019, T2020, G2021, C2022, L2023, V2024, Li2025, S2026, Sa2027, Ca2028, Aq2029, P2030
Anticipated reversals occur in unanticipated locations: avoid planar surfaces. As Saturn and Pluto come into alignment, prepare for irrepressible nostalgia. Casual attachments provide a medley of diversions from long-term fantasies. Mix of sulfur and magnesium is at its height on the 12th and 29th: stay clear of disarticulating headwinds while remaining open to miscalibrated address. Seek pine- and coconut-flavored dishes. Preferred alcohol: Anisette (neat).

T19, G20, C21, L22, V23, Li24, S25, Sa26, Ca27, Aq28, P29, A30
Reach out to long-estranged family members to say *life is better without you*. Don't back away from regrets. Outer Andromeda is fragmenting into deep time shallows: Time to stop the ambivalence and say *no*. Mid-month is best time for buying short but avoid other financial transactions. Look over your back before making sudden move. Avoid disco. Linger in

crinoline. Seek wool products and avoid rayon. Preferred alcohol: Pisco (sour).

G19, C20, L21, V22, Li23, S24, Sa25, Ca26, Aq27, P28, A29, T30
Pegasus wars with Orion, but zones of calm when Pyxis is rising. Smells intensify in arboreal regions. Old lovers come to mind, posing immediate threat. Keep eyes on interstitial aggravations. Tumeric and clove in seventh and thirteenth weeks will ward off transvirtual infection. Travel southward when possible but not before 6am local time. Persons from Uruguay will offer gift: not necessary to return favor but wait one week before opening. Seek volcanic dust. Preferred alcohol: Koskenkorva (with bitters).

C19, L20, V21, Li22, S23, Sa24, Ca25, Aq26, P27, A28, T29, G30
Turbulence in the nebula. Dark Matter in retrovariance. Take only third offers. Dress in chartreuse on even-numbered days and in mute orchid on odd days. Friendships cement in near term on days with "3" (3, 13, 30, 31) but stay at sea level on days with "5" (5, 15). Your horse will "place" on "0" days (10, 20, 30). Moods conform with waning and waxing moon, great calm at new moon. Avoid sexual contact at full moon. Seek bougainvillea. Preferred alcohol: Slivovitz (with orange peel).

L19, V20, Li21, S22, Sa23, Ca24, Aq25, P26, A27, T28, G29, C30
Turn no one away. Gold is buried just beyond shoreline. Emotional tides are uneven, but stay with them or undercurrent will pull you down. Magnetic fields from the melting polar caps run roughshod over love life. Avoid newspapers in second weeks; at other times start with recipes, when available. Jupiter crosses Saturn in perfect Equinity Semblance: keep measured distance from newcomers. Saturn is lodestar whose course tracks in avoirdupois: pound for feckless, dram for egress, stone for gravitation. Seek cantilevers. Preferred alcohol: Aguardiente (over ice)

V19, Li20, S21, Sa22, Ca23, Aq24, P25, A26, T27, G28, C29, L30
"The seraph / Is satyr in Saturn, according to his thoughts" (Wallace Stevens). Close call becomes near miss. Bounty holds only when seared. Jade is talisman of recusal and redaction. Aspiration punctuates lunar flares. Retreat in hollow days, parry on pivots. "The genius of misfortune / Is not a sentimentalist": defy writ to rend. The tally is incendiary, but fortune comes in buckets. Disable charms to charm. The following day

rips away the scuff of last. Cleave to presenting, adjacent insistence deems purpose. Seek such sentiment (not sentimental). Preferred alcohol: Drambuie (splits).

Li19, S20, Sa21, Ca22, Aq23, P24, A25, T26, G27, C28, L29, V30
Cold mouth, hot lips. Perpetuate fevered state, outlives livid transiencies. Dig hard but cede ground. Solar flares quash unspoken dreams but open path for development. Meteor showers in the south inflate currency. Lucky numbers: 8, 13, 331. Orient Eastward for repose, Westward for reflection. Scent: basil. Keep cool, under 60 degrees F., on first and last days of every month except first and last months. Eat soup weekly, alternating hot and cold. Seek predisposition. Preferred alcohol: moonshine (with rum).

S19, Sa20, Ca21, Aq22, P23, A24, T25, G26, C27, L28, V29, Li30
Watch for mid-Pacific squalls. Stay totally clear on such days. Even the smallest thought can betray you. Confide only in friends from past five years and only about matters that occurred over that time. Signs of incompatibility include swift and frequent eyelid clatter, extravagant hand motion, and midday drowsiness. Signs of compatibility include sudden rain, heightened gait, and tender elbow. High risk of falling into dark matter. Vigilance pays off on 3rd, 12th, and 19th day. Seek vermillion. Preferred alcohol: Trappist brandy (spritz).

Sa19, Ca20, Aq21, P22, A23, T24, G25, C26, L27, V28, Li29, S30
"What is most full seems empty. Yet its use will never fail. What is most straight seems bent. The greatest skill seems like clumsiness. The greatest eloquence like stuttering." (*Tao Te Ching*) Climb to the tallest point within your reach then lie flat at the lowest point, saying these words. Saturn's rings surround your despair: have courage! Sing a song of childhood when you feel farthest from it. Every crack of thunder speaks with the voice of your dearest lost loves. Seek oak. Preferred alcohol: rice wine (chilled).

Ca19, Aq20, P21, A22, T23, G24, C25, L26, V27, Li28, S29, Sa30
Settled matters unravel: time to take the advantage. Tropical depressions complicate unfamiliar liaisons, providing opportunities for needed adventure. Catch a falling star and put it in your pocket. Uranus rising: auspicious for small-bore improvements but not major renovation. Act as

if "there is no use in a center" (Stein): galvanize desire against regret and regret against compulsory well-being. Bird song provides big tip on holiday parties. Seek negative velocity. Preferred alcohol: mescal (with lemon).

Aq19, P20, A21, T22, G23, C24, L25, V26, Li27, S28, Sa29, Ca30
Sharp descent of Calypso Cluster drags Marmolean Veil into direct imbrication. Lucky numbers -6, -18, -871. Lucky colors: maroon, dead-island blue, mustard gray. Stay pressurized: do not leave capsule. Pseudoglossia is music from outer spheres but do not interpret or translate. Live in, not for, the moment. Seal the deal (resistance is a form of divination). Seek adjacency. Preferred alcohol: cachaça (with lime and sugar).

P219, A20, T21, G22, C23, L24, V25, Li26, S27, Sa28, Ca29, Aq30
Let envy propel you to eternity. Otherwise, duck and cover. Orion lays bare prognosis: structure treatment in response. Anxiety cools to fermenting antagonism: perpetuate memorialization. Sylvan linings pocket outsize payouts. Scatter in flutter, halt, then heave hard. Use thyme and ginger on 6th and 8th days of month, otherwise paprika (except in first and last days). Time will stand still at last moment. Follow the radiant sound of whoosh and whap. Declare insolvency as metaphysical foundation: blur affinities and self-identifications. Mid-months probe deep into shadows: reject false bottoms. Seek inardency. Preferred alcohol: absinthe (with Bénédictine).

Charles Borkhuis
United States

Tensile Strength
deeply embedded in road tongue
I give you the bumpy night on a silver spoon
what more can a grace note do
but run the next thought into ground-sparks
lipstick traces ooze circles 'round a wound
graffiti breath across the galaxy
makes your face shine in my spitball light

every empty socket is another pool shark's pocket
let's enter the great game and let winter flakes
fly off us like a fabulous new disease
don't lose me to a momentary backfire
I'm not your second-storey man
anonymous masked bandit trying to steal
a little fresh air from an unused planet

sure I'm scared to stare past the nothing hour
my mind loses its train its compartmentalized
brain and rolls into sky-crackling thunder
my shadow burned into a brick wall
my body electric ignites photons underfoot
no doubt you'll pick me out of a lineup
when my fever flashes poetic license

and darkness unloads its candles
I entered you from the other side of the milky way
suffice it to say I've grown light years older
but my bones can still manage a slow watusi
just to let you know it's me take a chance
on the shine off these wilting subway roses
give me a sign and I'm halfway there

Sunset Boulevard
my only chance to be someone
was to be someone else

no doubt there is contradiction at the core
take this face for instance
I won't be using it anymore

oh I could have saved it
like all the other stand-ins
oiled and shined it up
like a harvest moon
but I didn't have the heart

instead I threw it

to the sweetest dog I knew
who devoured it ravenously

but I still have two eye sockets
two nose hollows and a mouth hole
buried in a mask

better than ashes and diamonds
thrown on a coffin
better than a sticky silicon smile

I must admit I didn't look like myself
the way they'd fixed me up
I wouldn't have recognized me
passing on the street

Phantom Lips
they all said you can't have your mind
and eat it too
but what have we to nibble on in the wee hours
if not our own thoughts
those odd stirrings of an undigested world
that stick in our craw

the cannibal's dance at closing time
the uninvited guests who've come to dine
upon the fine bones of our inner ear
their phantom lips talk to us as we drowse
over the melting words in a book

I speak of course of the words that aren't there
the disjointed characters and snippets of scenes
the deformed faces that stare back at us
the folding chair that mimics the mouth
the broken hammer head and knowing smile
the buzzing lightbulb and wired jaw

wintry clouds breathe over these hands
the mercy twins tap dance in flowing nightgowns

as the antler-men tiptoe between wintery pines
listening to the blind woman's stick
that talks to stones a moment before sleep

maybe you've seen these wily tricksters
and confidence men who bubble up in tidepools
perhaps you've admonished the dog that barks at ghosts
and glimpsed the naked woodsman's shoulder
that spells out *mother where are you*
or the crows that peck breadcrumbs out of your hair
while erasing all memory of your journey

let us not forget the grand piano balanced on a rusty nail
that compels us to suddenly begin to spin
past our own morphing portrait on a wall as if
my face held the diaspora of millions under its dozing lids

as if when a hand squeezes a lover's shoulder
a leopard's eyes are illuminated through jungle leaves
and someone in a party hat is moved to confess
"my thoughts are not my own" and everyone laughs
while a stranger for no apparent reason
mumbles that further south shrunken heads are worn
on necklaces that speak omens to their owners

the mind is game to such unannounced visitations
the speckled salmon caught in a delirious leap of desire
the mockingbird that calls you by name
just in time to see your beloved palm trees uprooted
and flying away like colored flags
like old friends dead but still talking

the pieces in your hand don't fit
they're from another puzzle
buried inside another game
but oh so captivating all the same

Bulletproof
go scream your face off

go egg-blind suck the light off a bulb
won't do you any good
me neither
we're both looking for a simple grace note
a thought before it settles into a word
or the lump of a person
that instant when the stones in a stream murmur
never born . . . never die

and we both jump off a bridge into another body
the you inside me the pre-thought
bouncing off the rock face
no translation necessary
is this love
or are my feet pointed in the wrong direction

brains splatter abstract squiggles
intimates grow baby teeth branching fingers small flames
years of twining and whining separately or together
hands on the table
so no one gets away with murder
so drink me milky moonlight backflip

I'm calling your bluff she said
you're nothing but an ape in space
holding a bed in the palm of your hand
already my eyelids are getting heavy
count backwards he said
slowly from ten to one
one being unconditional love
then tell me you mean it for the thousandth time

who escapes the word's headlights
billboard prophecies playing across my shoe
they'll make a movie of us yet
robbing banks in our eighties
bulletproof we'll tiptoe across the constellations
you'll be an overnight sensation
so what if meaning catches up with us in the end

we'll have lived before our teeth begin to rattle

a baby's bullethead comes in various sizes
squeezing through a scream canal
too much to remember how we got here
empty as two so we may later lean
into each other's closed eyes
and dangle our legs over the great abyss
do a perilous two-step
that keeps the body in situation
breathless as it were
the dance of a scrap of newspaper in the wind
before words settle into things
the me inside you
holding on by a thread

Peter Boyle
Australia

The Joys of Mathematics
At fifty I will begin my count towards the infinite numbers.

At negative ninety-nine I will start my walk towards the
infinitessimally small.

At one over twenty-seven I will inspect the first bridgeworks.

At twenty two over seven I will write a message in a bottle, entrust
it to a sea turtle, slip under a wave and sleep.

At eighty-seven sparrows will land on the windowsill, pecking a
hole that leads inside my arm.

At 127 I will begin to arrange the children's pillows, carefully
filling each one with warm handfuls of snow.

At ten to the negative six our friends from the White House will

arrive,handing out glass beads and broken shells filled
with recently perfected poisons.

At the inverse square of sixteen the sky will curve over blue lakes,
songbirds settle at dusk, a small train rattle off towards a
village that leans against a single church spire.

At one over negative twenty-two I will start to dream in Sanskrit,
creating a swarm of brown ants to bring back a baby's
rattle from the edge of a mud slide.

At ten to negative two over three I will open my heart, letting go
of all vanities, right down to the wilted bones.

At the third transfinite number I will give up easy answers.

At e to the i pi the earth will bristle with skulls and weapons,
dolphins will proclaim the first inter-stellar arms bazaar
in Antarctica, the new born will drink only lead, the
elderly will wander the moon in the quest for warmth.

At one I will open my eyes.

At zero I will put the key back under the mat.

Missing Words

I don't know how many things there are in this world that have no name.
The soft inner side of the elbow, webbed skin between the fingers, a day
that wanders out beyond the tidal limits and no longer knows how to
summon the moon it has lost, my firstborn who gazes about himself when
the TV dies and there is a strange absence in his world. I was looking for
a great encyclopaedia, the secret dictionary of all the missing words. I
wanted to consult its index and find out what I could have become. The
sound the clock makes when it is disconnected and taken down from the
wall but can't lose the habit of trying to jerk itself forward. The look of
old socks drying on a rack in the kitchen all through a winter night,
hanging starched and sad opposite the wedding photographs. A word for
your face when you know you can't love but would almost like to try. The
blurred point of merger between fresh storm damage to a house and the

deep fissures that have always been there. Walking down the corridor to the front door with inexplicable elation in my chest as if everything was about to start, as if my love had just arrived, escaped from a burning world, and at the same time clenched in my taut wrists, my hands, the thin bones of my arms, the certainty that everything has long been over.

Jerry Bradley
United States

The Island of the Dolls
The sons of ancient cultures
take legends seriously, and secretive men
respect simple signs: when an eagle perched
on a cactus in the middle of a dying lake,
the first Aztec souvenir was born.

Escaping Mexico City's sprawl for the afternoon,
we board a non-motorized trajinera and pay the boatmen
to pole us through the Xochimilco canals
where the last reported axolotls live. The craft's
floral arches are as ornate as the gaudy gates of heaven.

Soon a barge of mariachis draws near;
one extends his sombrero for tips,
as an enfilade of vendors speeds
close behind to fox us out of our cash.
Just like the salamanders, we are gringos on our own.

The best-known of the floating chinampas
is Isla de las Muñecas, the Island of the Dolls,
where a loner once fished the body of a drowned girl
from the water. The next day a doll washed up,
and he hung it from a branch. Today

dozens of broken bodies, some decapitated,
others with severed limbs, adorn the trees and fences.
Their soulless eyes are always open, haunt the place;

rumors fly like the whispers of wailing women.
Only the charmed can see the first sign of madness.

Beauty and the Beast

A rich merchant had three daughters, all of them gorgeous,
Especially the youngest whom everyone called Beauty.
But when the merchant lost his fortune in the Bitcoin collapse,
He lost most of his property except for a small cottage
Where he tilled the lavender fields; as he did, Beauty looked after
The house while her sisters lay in bed reading screen magazines
And grumbling about their lost wealth.

When the merchant heard that a semi containing
Overdue goods was on its way, the family was excited.
He met the truck at the loading dock to receive the cargo,
But his creditors were there too, and he returned home
As poor as when he'd left. He ached to remember the fine suits
He once wore, how he once admired himself in the looking glass.

We know how the story goes. To save her father,
Beauty shacked up with a prosperous but hideous beast.
She tried to find something in him to admire,
But a fellow can't be ugly his whole life and not be affected
In an unseemly way. So one night at bedtime she placed
Her ring on the table and left, having learned the hard way
That many a monster has the shape of a man.

Belling the Vampire

Forget the cats and upland buzzards you'll see after nuclear war,
the low oaths you mutter into your tankard that will not work.
He wants a mouthful of your milk-pink lemonade
and a moonlight waltz, but, if you don't want to dance
in his deep-vein jamboree, buy yourself a glove
and an aluminum bat. Oh, sure, garlic is tasty and great
for enchiladas in mole, but one clove won't be enough,
and chants and incantations work about as well.
Get yourself a tiny brass bell. Call it self-defense
and call this a letter from an unhinged friend,
but, when you hear its tinkle, it will sound like the siren

58

of something surprising approaching in a mach-one spurt,
astonishing and as startling as seeing a gar in the bathtub, a white guy
making change at the U-Totem, or the pope in a Hawaiian shirt.

Mischance
Where the truck went off the road
there are the dark marks
of tarskid wheels on pavement,
a retaining post knocked aside,
a simple version of disaster
visible now in the patrolman's flare.
Say there was a woman in the shadows he saw,
a shape whose branchy arm gave sign,
or suppose the hooks and eyes of night
called from obsidian thickets like sex
this can happen! this can happen!
Believe his rig in flatbed fury
tore him over the embankments of nighttime lust,
a wife ahead, kids asleep,
and brought him brow on glass
where siren howl the spot
short of home   dead.
Rate excessive, he missed the turn;
the report says he ignored the sign,
just some Saturday accident,
a routine weekend mishap,
nothing special and too late
for the Sunday pages

A Field Guide to Dreams
a man owes something to his dreams

waking in the strange night or shivering in a stream,
he is blind beyond the curve where the hyacinth gathers

and the river becomes a boring stretch of road
its curve is like the curve of her leg

and when in sleep you swim

59

the long shadow upstream to her
and away from the sneer of fish
you become something orchestral

the water trembles
as you dance in the oyster wash

and waves crack
like broken sidewalk around you

before day comes
and you resort to common life again

this morning when I opened my dream box,
all there was was the moon

John Bradley
United States

Placental Gravity

I was born in a box of Cheerios, inside the pantry, near the broom and the
bison.
I was born in my mother's armpit, her stubbly flesh smelling of a pickle
barrel.
I was born behind a common comma, mapping out the whirling world of
my coma.
I was breathing through the pores in my feet, pouring out a fog which
would later say, *Edgar Allen Poe poured whiskey on his Wheaties.*
I was born with my head in my mouth, tongue in my brain, my blood
pounding this refrain: *All languages merge into a single
incomprehensible language.*
I closed my eyes, stars burning through my eyelids, so many stars I knew
they had to be ridden and riddle.
I closed my eyes, and I could see Walt Whitman humping a support beam
on the Brooklyn Bridge, Herman Melville in the planetarium huffing
whale blubber, Emily Dickinson in a black veil scrawling her birth
name on the belly of a tomato worm.

I was breathing through every line and stanza I had yet to write, words
    floating just above and below the colon in my heart, telling me,
    Unbind yourself from the hands of the clock, even as the numbers
    blister, as they snap, crackle, pop.
I was breathing in all the cigarette smoke I would ever choke on,
    mulching it into dead leaves.
My first words were *Hello, Placental Gravity. Hello, Slug in the Coffee*
    Can Soaking in Kerosene.
My first words were *Everyone, take to your bomb shelter now. Leave*
    behind your welts and shredded wheat.
I was, I was, and yet I was not yet born. This all happened when it will
    happen, only then and now.
No, I was born on the back of a velvet ant, wearing a tin crown. Laden
    with Lucky Charms.

For Joyce Mansour, Lost in Cairo
Every third window. You said
I could find you in Cairo behind
every third window. A smoking pipe
filled with red sand. A cat with a bandaged
tail. A lizard that speaks in a tongue
heard only from a damp wrist.

You carry a violin case, but you won't
tell me what's inside. I write
on your wrist: *In Cairo, the moon*
possesses glass teeth. You laugh.
An onion rolls across the street.
Who placed that bandage
at the base of my spine
while I was asleep?

Behind every third window
I find twenty-three grains of sand.
You tell me to gather them
in an envelope. Mail them back
to you. But you left no address

on my wrist. Only the drawing

of an ibis. Much too hungry.

Before My First, After My Last, I Wear Dirt's Shirt
That shirt I buried belonged to my father, his lifespan of breathing dirt. I
didn't care that the shirt would remain alive and alert in the dirt. Oh, to
dig a shirt out of the earth and wear it for a little while above the dirt. It
wasn't that the shirt had had relations with some malodorous dirt. I
should let the dirt bury whatever it wants to bury in the dirt. *Dirt to dirt*, I
said over the hole in the earth, *shirt to shirt*. As we all know, a shirt
should never be worn by shapeless or even shapely dirt. I should never
have listened to those holes eating the collar of the shirt. I buried the shirt
because . . . because all around me there was so much dirt. I should not
have let something that commingled with skin commingle with dirt. I
don't really want to know what happens when dirt begins to inhabit a
shirt. I've buried the ashes of a sickly cat, a contaminated book, but never
a still breathing shirt. If only I'd listened to the sky and let the shirt
expire in a tree like withered dirt. And if the shirt should rise up and flail
its flimsy arms, flinging loose pebbles and dirt? Oh, to fall to the dirt and
vanish at the same moment as your earthly shirt.

Roundlet: From the *Book of Arrested Propulsion*
And the people made of ash would eat
only ants made of wood, and the people

made of wood would eat only lizards
made with lightning, and the people

made of lightning would eat only
the flesh of the people made of ash.

Zoe Brooks
United Kingdom

There's Nothing to See
I have taken off my body
and hung it on the wardrobe door.
It has become too much for me.
I am tired of pulling it on

each morning rumpled by sleep

I have worn it so long
it has lost its shape.
Threads have caught and drawn,
patches rubbed bare,
each fold a place for shadows to hide.

I pass the mirror in the hallway
and there's nothing to see,
nothing to catch on the parquet floor
nothing to mark the doormat,
as I walk outside.

Dorothy Wilson Said

Dorothy Wilson said
if you swung hard enough
you would go in a circle
right over the apple branch.
But I knew she was lying.
I knew the jolt at the top,
that suspense before falling back,
the disappointment.

After Dorothy Wilson left for Wales,
I swung so hard
I flew over the Black Mountains
to the sea.

Sue Burge
United Kindom

It Only Happens In My Dreams

The Hollywood Hills are full of cats. One, dark as a puddle,
follows you home, chews your fingertips till they bleed.
Offer him milk, cream, a splash of brandy. Wake in the night,

see him poised on claws as sure as pointe shoes,
his shadow on the ceiling, your dreams in his mouth.

Confess to the prophetic cowboys with their singing spurs,
ask them to write you a paranormal "to do" list.
They will take your hands in their buckskin palms,
counsel you in fuzzy, faraway voices.

The Hollywood Hills are full of pickpockets with no pasts,
their eyes flicker like headlights on a slattern sky, zombie
tongues lolling with lust for the contrail of your memories.
Run higher, higher still, to the sign that once said Hollywoodland,
swing like Douglas Fairbanks from the top of the Y.
Roll, roll down the dry, heaving sides of Mulholland Drive.
The Hollywood Hills are full of lies.

I am writing this underwater
but it is not my last will and testament. My toes are tucked, neat and
patient, under the rim of a chalkreef. My hair held back with a band of
thrice-wrapped bladderwrack. My notebook is waterlogged and
waterproof. My pen has a strange heft. Sometimes my words escape.
When I weep, my tears are carried slow and far as starlight. My clothes
do not contain the weighty pockets you might expect. Some day I will be
raised by the blind sweeping of a trawler net, limbs barnacled, lips blue
with prophesy:

oh cool peaty seas
    awash with tied line and cages
all poised palaver and melting camber
    you wither our bygone earth
leave us brittle core
    let us palm poems
on the scaly tails of wildlings
    let us lullaby mothersong:

> *my mother is not the wings*
> *but the rhythm and the darkness*
> *not the wings*
> *but the sinew and gristle that holds*

each crunch of bone
each sip of marrow
she is not the wings
but the struggle for flight
dragging cold blind storyskin
across rising waters

*"my mother is not the wings" is the first line of *c'mon* by Ross Gay

Rachel Burns
United Kingdom

Behind the Scenes at the Museum
Nobody saw him peel off the layers
to the skeleton beneath.
Nobody saw the skin shed
like a coat to the floor.
And the road signs
pointing the wrong way.
The fruit bowls with their shiny plastic fruit -
the skeleton stood like the grim reaper
over the new-born. Eighty tall red vases
appeared. Seventy-nine
made cheaply in a factory in China
one hand painted in England
with 18- carat gold.

Black Butterflies
June and the black butterflies
are hatching from their chrysalides.
We watch him play a tune
on a blade of grass, black flies
thicken the air.

The children sing to the baby
push the old pram, with the squeaky
wheel, up and down, up and down.
The baby is screaming, snot and tears.

We sit on the newly washed white step,
it stinks of bleach. The children play
leapfrog, hopscotch, skipping games.

Words fall from his mouth
like broken teeth.

Casey Bush
United States

horsekicked
Forgive the whole world in advance. The ignorant speak about things of
which they know little or nothing. Rancid bladderwort. Myopic
kaleidoscope. The sage remains silent but then writes a book to explain
his thoughts. Buzzcut survivor. Ukulele war bonnet. Been using LSD to
develop my ESP. Candle extinguished by an ocean breeze. Rustle of my
dress before the dance. Lone passenger disembarks at a whistle stop.
Light's gone out at the end of the tunnel. Television reception gets
worse after midnight. Paying interest on borrowed time. Single wink of
the cockcrow. Hammer pounding on an anvil inside my eardrum.
Joyous laughter of a prime number which has yet to be discovered.
Another tomato from Altoona. The soothsayer is widely quoted but his
predictions are commonly misunderstood. Although living in obscurity I
keep busy every day.

helixoid
Weary of the Bardo? Tired of this powder room Purgatory? Our journey
through life is one slow turning wheel. Bloodied fingers pound the piano
demanding answers. Angels speak to me but with a foreign accent.
These handcuffs are cutting off my circulation. Throw another log on the
fire. Herein lies the hitch. Worrying about problems only makes matters
worse. Take a step back as a crazed nun rampages through the Vatican
gift shop, debating scripture with a lava lamp, desperate for an abortion.
Such a muddle over what can easily be found in any child's pants pocket:
rusty jackknife, compass without a needle, candy melted inside the
wrapper, balloon drained of air, corner piece of a jigsaw puzzle, rainbow

split in half. Let's dream once more whether or not it's time to turn out the lights.

Garrett Caples
United States

Targets and Flowers
(begun with lines from André Breton)

Sometimes she turns around in the printed seasons and asks the time, or even pretends to look jewels straight in the eye.

Sometimes she gets her bearings from watchmakers, her hardness from the balance-beam, as she bends to pull a stocking up.

Sometimes she glances into mirrors, impressing onto unglazed surfaces imagined permanence.

Sometimes she appears in the center of something circular—targets and flowers—and hurriedly adjusts her hair.

Sometimes she speaks in mascara.

Sometimes she clasps an hourglass between her legs and slows time to a trickling waltz, or writes her signature across an hour's measure.

Sometimes, when she's "in vogue," she walks abroad in search of the *Herald-Tribune*, and people throw coins and gum and fruit, mistaking her for the Russian dancer with the wintry smile and clandestine desires.

Sometimes she removes the flares from the modern mode, and brings forth objects stout and stiffened with stove-enamel.

Sometimes she reverses the tweedle and tintinnabulation into a giddy spiral of music, translating somersaults with a turn of the lathe into smooth and careless gestures.

Sometimes she sparks these gyrations.

Untitled

Imagine a town with no numbers. Did I say *a town*? I more meant *expanse* of unplanned plains, or optional intersections. Fields, some trees. No commerce, of course, no work 'cept for food, and who wants to eat alone? (I picture spontaneous picnics.) *The individual* is still accepted, *hate* is not unknown, but demand for solitude's grown so rare we lacked concepts for its expression. *She wants to be with herselves*, let's say, or even, *with the trees*. Where? Over there, for we lost track of North and South. The sun doesn't rise so much as light surrounds us until we ascend into night. We killed people, it's true, to adjust their attitude, but could you have lived in their town? A house that was eating itself before it was even home? My bed was in the fireplace. Porcelain cats are cold. Blood seeps under the ballroom floor where the creature bit off its sex. They never found it; the ground swallowed. Now people can lay on the grass and dream. The mountains are anywhere the reclining journey begins. Gorge on its purple pines. Squint at the church of obsidian ribs hidden in its chest. Horses pour from one another. Their skulls branch over the living quarter. The town might appear in a grave rubbing, its sky no void but cataract. Those tears of eros look like diamonds but taste like shit, and they cut the world's oval throat in a delicate squirt of hibiscus. The tiny blots that spatter blossom into little birds.

"i have seen enough"

inside his apartment where he and i smoked the roach of his age and my youth for the first time since he died, examining his papers. as if on cue the toilet explodes. ("the plumbing is victorian," he'd say, apologetically, instructing a guest not to flush; only he had the right touch.) "i have seen enough," written on a page dated 7 years, 2 days before his death. the odor of the place clings to my clothes, the way it pervaded his books, a compound of tobacco and indefinable fragrances. for the rest of the day i attract birds: pigeons roost on my lap; a rooster runs by; a quartet of wild parrots buzz me mid-thigh at high speed. all this in downtown san francisco. surreality is real. even a sparrow nearly bumps into me. another sits next to me, contemplating me. she tells me a story. they were walking in a park when they saw two kildeer mating in the grass suddenly swallowed by a lawnmower, and here are the letters he wrote to the superintendent of parks, and the poems against the lawnmower. sometimes the pages seem effortless, stretching into passages exuberant and harrowing. there were years he didn't write, yet you'd never know seeing his papers arranged in decades. these are poet's ashes, volcanic and smoldering still. to lose this scent is to enter permanent exile.

for Nancy J. Peters & Philip Lamantia

Love Is Made of Sky

love is a movie we watch ourselves in, a film we wash ourselves in. a sky that looks askance at the lack of scandalousness in even the most licentious thought. the song of the beleaguered dispatcher herding taxis together, or the hiss of inflatable ramps sliding down desire. love is a cloud in the sky that's also love. i remember today like it was yesterday. i open a door and there stands love, ready to get down, and i'm like whoa, we just met and love's like i don't care. love has a history of such indiscretions. a baby wailing on an electric fivestring banjo during a piano recital in the library of a redeye flight to boston could no more disconcert than love when love comes to town on a fine arab charger or even a budweiser clydesdale. love drives whatever it wants and frankly prefers something furrier than the average fuzzy dice. the velvet cheesesteak applepie of the snowbound vermont mind is dismissed by love as missing the point of the needle, its flawless tenderness and penchant for cool appraising stares below the roof of its woolhat horizon. love instead noodles nile delta blues at 79 rpms. the rpgs of love explode at the antipodes of saint dope island and carnal canal, for love wreaks magic havoc with the music of public life. love loves it when love does it because love is a moonlit boxing glove giving the finger to violence. a sky we look upon that mumbles and falls, and a bright blue sun in the sky. love is a risky sky.

Paul Bowles in El Cerrito

rhe marimbas and the marijuana were the only good things in the town. the men were violent and dirty. the women were made of stone. a tortilla might run up and smack your face. the doilies were straight unforgivable. there was a cactus the size of the grand cooley dam and a pencil the size of a lizard. a burro made of churros and a pinata stuffed with opinions. compared to my life as a mountain dweller, even the bums were city slickers. the wind always blew hard and cold. the marijuana and arhoolie records were the only good things in the town. there were ill-mannered goats as big as great danes, while the great danes themselves were like runty chihuahuas. the university presses were nothing to speak of and the abandoned monasteries less than picturesque. the palm trees were clenched like fists. the guitars were out of tune and the pianos had 86 keys. it was illegal for men to breastfeed in public. the ample parking and the marijuana were the only good things in the town. the flowers gave off the most foul odor. the sex offenders barely registered. there were no gas stations and it was a pain in the ass to go to the dentist. the internet was a broken wheel propped against a well, the telephone a buzzard on a shed. there were neon signs like giant banana leaves and stick bugs like you wouldn't believe. the gorge that lay below the town yawned and belched a puff of smoke, because the marijauna and the barbeque were the only good things in the town.

for Andrew Joron and Rose Vekony

Srinjay Chakravarti
India

At the Sleepwalkers' Hotel
Because the margins will finally rise/ over their edges/ and drown the text.// I stopped over at the sleepwalkers' hotel.
—Tomas Tranströmer, The Gallery

We wade through an avenue of shadows,
blades of black grass
which cling to our footprints
           like wet tar.

The faces of the dead,
shaping the wallpaper
into Noh masks,
    Inca mummies,
    Saqqara casts.

Fingers read the braille
  on engraved pillars,
petrified trees holding up a forest sky
        with hieroglyphs carved
          on wood and stone.

Windows are rusted grids,
        trellised metal

sieving starlight,
                        rain,
and memories.
On their graphs,
we plot the asymptotes
        where horizons meet.

The future comes back
                        to haunt us,
        extrapolations of plotted curves
in hyperbole and ellipsis.

Daily almanacs for our journeys,
    voyages down corridors
    where carpets are plush
        with adulteries
and even original sins are vicarious.

        But these here are doors opening
                        into themselves,
        a succession of mirrors
through which we see our other selves,
                        darkly.

This is the way we must return,
        our rooms tenanted by dreams
        moving in rhythm
            with the custodians
            of night's blindness:
vampire bats, screech owls, ghosts, and zombies.

        Through the scented garden
        and its treadmill of aloneness,
our footsteps take us to the well,
        deep with decay,
    where liquid darkness pools
                in an abyss of oblivion.

        This is where we fall,

deep into inky water,
coming up only for air,
into light,
into waking,
into language.

Lidia Chiarelli
Italy

Land of Magic
...All of this in time suspended
The universe holding its breath
There is a hush in the air...
Lawrence Ferlinghetti

In the land of magic
we wander on the paths
of an unknown world.

Magritte's eyes
floating in the clouds

the empty, glaucous orbits of Modi

Marilyn's dreamy, tired eyes

all astonished look around.
We pause and listen to
their silent message
then
sinking deeper into a spiral of colors
are slowly captured
by a strange
whirling
dance.

Graham Clifford
United Kingdom

Crossing
My brother started crossing animals with kitchen implements, garden furniture, screws, nuts, bolts, fixings, ironmongery and work wear, guttering and drainage solutions, door and window fittings, Hi Vis overalls, fillers, aggregates and sealants, work towers and cleaning essentials.

He raised a half hedgehog half old-fashioned tape measure. He was very pleased with the snakes that part-way along fanned out as all the sizes of Allen key.

They would be reared in ice cream tubs, an old chest freezer or on his bottom bunk. And all the animal/objects weren't obviously upset by their uniqueness in the world. My brother could manage pain with the skill of an anaesthetist.

Our parents asked him about pursuing his crossing as a proper career but he wouldn't hear of it.

A sparrow/whisk on his shoulder and a pocket alive with woodlice/Rawlplugs, he tried to tell me there was more to life than the obvious but I couldn't understand a word as his tongue was pimpled with the buttons off an ornate till and his motivation was insulated with a no nonsense and damp-resistant expanding sticky foam.

The Righteous Path
Then there were Jesuses everywhere. They crowded like water fleas in the supermarket and butted into lightbulbs at night like moths. One woman had a desiccated one set in a banned sort of resin and wore it as a broach. Every tiny tooth perfect in miniature; think yawning baby shark.

A really big one decided its job was to stand on the horizon like an inaccurately beneficent history that everyone colludes with because of the way light congratulates the enormous, softening edges in a water-colour way.

Juggernauts would flatten them in their thousands on B-roads in the sweltering mating season and some teenagers kept them in boxes and grew attached to how their Jesuses made nests from rips of dead other Jesuses. How they would look mournful weaving legs.

You turned into Jesus and I say, It must be tiring. I know how hard it was just to be you, but now you are Jesus. You must find it difficult to juggle this and your family and work commitments.

Not at all, you say. It was like stepping into a warm room. As soon as I decided, I got this kit and the address to a website where I could dump my past. I got this enamelled badge and all this paperwork. Work have been fine, I'm now seen as a kind of mascot or lucky charm.

But you didn't mention your children, I say. Jesus didn't have kids, you reply.

The White Baboon
A white baboon became important.

Everyone visited the zoo to see what he had done to become important. He reflected everyone's life at the breakfast table back at them. Who could not be moved by the white baboon and his achievements?

He was also an excellent draftsman. Sometimes it was the tops of houses he could make out from his cage, or a visitor he remembered. A keeper bought him canvases to use the paints he had made using oil from Tapir excreta and rocks that children still threw at him.

By humanely removing the top of his skull, neuroscientists properly understood the white baboon's importance and helped us to. This success coincided with a dip in zoo ticket sales; attributable to the allowable and expected mid-implementation slump bought about by edgy economic policy.

There were no ill effects from his surgery or the subsequent analysis which involved sedated journeys to the best universities. They sold the research paper in the souvenir shop. At K. University he was allowed to dress in jeans and a t-shirt. The baboon was once beaten for an affair with a handler's wife.

The baboon went bald, grew back his hair, dreamt he was flying, dreamt of real places he'd never been to, and drew and drew and drew. He tattooed one of his peers with his own language and smashed three sons on a boulder near the tyre swing.

In summers, he was captivated by the skittish algorithm of sunny gnats. He understood.

Peter Lorre Bird
The parakeet
that reminds us of Peter Lorre
reaches from its aviary
but I don't let its talon
take my finger for a handshake
or a friendly tug.
It is needy
like a beaten dog,
a small hunk of life
grown so skilful in coercing
we balk and instead
I proffer my water bottle.

It bends to the fencing
and in order to reach further out
turns its head
so it is looking away
which seems like
sickened but bankrupt compliance.

It takes the cap in its grip
and gently, blindly unscrews.

Brian Clifton

United States

Scarlet Heaven

An Itoh peony begins as an eye—it awakens. The yellow petals peel from
the vibrating pupil. On screen, it blinks. A bulb of worry, a brain
consuming itself. How much does a pixel cost the environment? Who will
see it moving and the burning behind its movement? The flower's red
mouth opens, and its worries shift around. Loose yellow teeth. The flower
tongues its yawning petals. It is so full of itself. Compressed like an organ
in a ribcage. The sutures loosen. Fire pours out its golden hair. The Itoh
peony is a drop of blood with an ember inside. It is a corpse on a
conveyor belt to a cremator—the flames glow within the square hole
across the concrete room. The flower spreads its bloodless wound. It
shows the yellow pearls of fat that glitter in the cremator's eerie light.
Maggots that sizzle into oil. A larger destruction whirs overhead. Lifting
away, the peony reveals inside itself a single room—an extended family
sitting around a table. The moving geometry of getting up, taking a spot,
coming back, quibbling over possession. Aunts and uncles writhe in
laughter. A child falls, is swarmed by other children. A parent points
outside. Someone leans in and remarks on death or the difficulty one
faces in the evening behind the screen trying to capture a bird in motion
above the tall grass. The Itoh peony pinches like a cul-de-sac. People file
into the street. Music, quiver. They talk about a recent storm, the power
outage that drained the city of resources. One by one streetlights
flickered. Then men in bright yellow vests came. They milled about their
trucks. They chainsawed the debris and carried it away. The city
reopened. How long can any catastrophe occupy? Today, highway traffic
flutters a petal outside while inside a peony, a pulsing border. The earth
dilates—white-filmed, bloodshot it looks at a screen where an Itoh peony
dulls out its red drone.

Apocalypse With Bed Sheets

My husband sleeps. In the garage, I smash the cans in the recycling. I
float into our room. He is a lump under the covers. I remember when he
destroyed the porch furniture with his maul. Each crack opened my eyes. I
pick him up, and he unravels into a sheet. I look out the window. My
husband scurries under the porch. He slips down the storm drain. *Good
riddance*, I think and tuck myself in.

Andrei Codrescu
United States

Any Habit
I will wear a monk's habit like Max Jacob.
I was murdered by nazis in the camps.
I am wearing a mask. They are gassing us.
The world is a concentration camp.
I can't breathe, nobody ever could.
I am wearing a mask. Jacob wore a habit.
"I love to lift it as I walk up the stairs."
We are creatures of habit, any habit.
We always wore masks. We always wore habits.
We will always be murdered by nazis.
We don't need any wisdom or foolishness.
The stairs go up and up like poison gas.

Textinction
something I made up
in the mirror of enmeshed languages

survived briefly then died

in my lifetime

it was poetry
it was art
it was the ineffable stench of a dying world

I speak two human languages

each one mirrored by its twin and followed by its echo

each word an abstracted world dying when it is spoken
followed by dreams and repetition

in the morning I make up the bed
I chase out bodies from the hollow
of repetition and the echo of mirrors that have looked deeply

into my sleep

strangers roomed there
they brought news to me
ripe fruit of words fallen on the ground ripe fruits of babel

before the despair of twilight
sets up the mirrors for another night daytime goes into another
        fleeting poem

that leaves behind shadow and echo

reader don't bother to learn these words
i am ishi the last speaker of this coiled wire

my mysterious languages buzz in mirrors inside and outside your
        homes
some of them are in your dreams

narcissus doesn't care where he sleeps he prefers wordless poetry
to vanishing mirrors polluted springs

absorbed by screens of forgetting

Love Song
"pneumonia is the old man' s friend"
was that for ages and it was nature suffocating you
with her own hands. "My time has come" the old
ones said. "It is my turn."

History is an uninterrupted row of disasters that kills with abandon and
with rage generations. We rightly mourn the young, but in old age we
know that the clock of the body quits keeping time.

Until recently that is, when our minds understood our bodies better and
began to keep the old clocks ticking until the rooms were full of us and air
hard to breathe.

Oh thinkers scientists tinkerers and entertainers longevity creators all we
thank you for keeping us here bored and dismayed and full of fear. The
beyond is

overpopulated and you never know what a reconstituted cadaver might
become, a feather, a worm or a vampyr.
If you are lucky what is "you" will contribute form
in the soup. The young will miss us until the will is read.
Personally I write sonnets so they'll say "he said."
I am still here as the plague rages. There is a doctor in my bed.
She hates my generation but likes me for some reason.

My generation was an ideology of naked angry youth
We left behind some language and found a common thread.

Let us leave now we did our damage. It is an alien season.

With Walter Benjamin in Queens
You can't make a new man but you can kill old ones Walter Benjamin in
Moscow 1927 noted posters exhorting the masses with the slogan "Time
Is Money" attributed to Lenin the only god the lazy Russians masses
pretended to listen to but did not no matter how big Majakovski made the
letters

New Man apexed in "Metropolis"
then the execution of prototypes was on.

Lenin like Chernishevski asked "what is to be done?"

Tramways sleds steel factories babies breast milk pioneers
Lenin and the The New Man capitalized themselves even in this poem
thanks to their monster babies spchk and auto-correct

Benjamin went to Moscow at the right time or just in time
to escape being an executed prototype or frozen in the tundra.

His timing served him by not being in New York either in 2020

a lucky man he wrote his thoughts and executed himself
he was the New Man after all not leninist not sci-fi a free man

The Frog Stanza
When I was a child I had no trouble destroying the world
with mind-rays. The neighbors who communalized our kitchen.
The empty ghost-houses in the overgrown bushes
behind the crumbling cement walls where ghouls screeched.
The stepfather who wrestled my dog Nemo out of my arms
and gave him away to someone I'm still looking for.
The classmate who tried to buy the frog stanza I didn't sell him.

Fathers, cities, trains, empty skies, the shadow police, school.
I was moody and destruction was the vivid product of my mind.
I observed ants and bees and wild cats and I was sad for them.
I was happy for the birds. I didn't know how cats destroyed them.
The clouds looked fluffy until they filled up with info instead of
            water.

Like stadiums they now belong to corporations they are going
            dark.

The politics are as bad as the environment gasping for breath.
We won't make it to that nitrous oxyde planet, friend.
We won't laugh involuntarily when our teeth and eyes are gone.

Walk like the goats, straight up, what is this rock for anyway?

Diana L. Conces
United States

Avatar
Pulling strings and fixing things
I see: two hands are not enough.
Digging in my flesh—I extract
a lump. I pull, shape, carve:
fashion my twin and send her
out into the world in my stead.

She wears a smooth mask; she does
precisely what is necessary.
She calculates the interest of the many.
　　　　—She is not real.—
All day they talk to my twin
and do not know it. They speak
my name; my avatar responds.

Slid

Just one tangerine dollop of yolk oozing,
thickly down the curved bowl of sky
trailing turmeric and cinnamon
to the inevitable dusk, lingering
in that elephant moment before
drowning in a million diamond
sparkles of dappled forgetfulness
on the gray sea. When the whiff
of seaweed penetrates the membrane
of that one, pure moment,
not only the seagulls find
answers in the crushing weight
of sunset where light and wisdom
pool together one taunting breath
before sliding into a restless slumber.

Alfred Corn
United States

Brush With Greatness

I got good at getting the hairs out of it,
grunt work, granted, but handled pdq.
The aftermath felt cozy, collaborative,
to the extent people ever looked at a flash
going off when the designated carpet salesman
drove up, a worm turned, or an avuncular type
winked and quipped, "You little so-and-so."

Kiwi had its points, so did peach, ditto

81

cocoa—and silver, especially old silver,
goes with any color, it's that versatile.
I could drink most of them most days.
They could also be instantly spewed out
when a fit of debunking took over.
.

You saw it first, the drunken wasp whose tail
got mistaken for a black-and-yellow barcode.
Consider it a childhood memory of parks.
In that dawn time everybody ran in packs,
so we called our gang The Bronx Luckies.
For mass transit the transported had to buy
brass tokens, a buck-ten each. They stuck it
to you, same way Chinese "cash" had piercings—
We're talking before plastic swallowed everything up.

And ever shall be. The clunker remaining?
It wasn't sex work, it was survival. Besides,
nothing never ends, even when it busts a few
killer moves trying to or when you card
a mom or any other fiber optic. Oh: would you tell
your friend odds are she'll be going home soon.

Alice's Rules
Any behavior even suggesting restraint
should expect a faceful of cream pie. Be free
or else. How'd they say do it? "Thanks, I've got
other plans," and, these put into effect, steal home,
veer off at a tangent, whatever, so you won't be
boxed in and made to fess up. Prefer the faux
marble urn to the "real," a malicious fake, and harp
on what was never thought but oft expressed
so as to convey the contraband being imported.
An offensive is most when delivered deadpan,
no mouthed butter melting as the loom is bowered.
"Know what I'm saying?" we say, hedging our bets
when we hog the mike, lest the players trip over
the ferns or refuse to use flamingos for their mallets.

Today man (or woman) is guaranteed to feel
a lot more like now than was true yesterday —
depending, granted, on which day we're talking
and on whose nickel. In the city of Dis, junkie
and disc-jockey smote the chest, crumpling
posies meant to impress the Empress with.
"Please come in and perch in front of my latest
mirror writing while we punt up the river Lapis,
whose surface dimples with parodic fleur-de-lis."
Collection amounts to a new *Fleurs du mal*?
They'll have to squawk and earn it first. Then be
proclaimed a touchdown, toast of the capital —
though still hard-pressed, a burn-victim of ironic
and amped-up malingerers. The loyals, meanwhile,
need to scrape together a little support, each two
of us pitching in, a-pelting ye olde dodos with sugared
almonds. Numbing out on a nemesis so manual as that,
what'll we ens and ems have to say for ourselves?

At Some Length
Engulfing warmth. Or else a cold well,
down to the walls and grainy margin,
the pulse of darkening guesswork
forgotten since, but now dredged up:
ionized ambient dissonance,
drumbeats of darkened guesswork bent
on entering some null not-there, plumbed to
a depth where stunned agos still make the rules.

But first, the last selving eruptions—
avid, eristic, molten—to foreshadow
a starved trek to their conclusive DMZ.
Archeological digs, intent
on disturbing finds that might be lifeless
but also, in a closer light, unkillable.

Cheiromancy
The Roma hung on each word of those stories
you could tell, surprised not to have become

83

the "out" that no-trespassing signage keeps.
Palmistry will interpret what resembles
a landscaped enchiridion, sentences scored in
by manual labor and deep enough today
to draw blood. Yet if dig-we-must types need
a dozen stamens (or a baker's dozen) before
getting to stamina, still they'll want to master
a language in which "joy" also means "music."
Couldn't you watch with me at least one hour?
A waterdrop swells, dangles from the eaves,
trembles, but doesn't fall; then falls with several
followers falling after. Quick days unfurl
before the thaumaturge stops short to gauge
ice clouds that he says promise "feathered rain."

It comes down to reverse sublimity,
Joseph: the void within the dark within the silence
that instills your snowfield's zero choirs.
At dawn, a single mallard loping across the sky,
Nature's own page-turner. Who knows how long
ago that picture stopped living in the future.

Painstaking surveys of our northern forests,
tungsten mines or a strung loom start feeling
like love, potlatch or fresh-plowed farmland.
"For being ignorant to whom it goes,
I writ at random, very doubtfully."
Will that mean drydocking the barnacled
clipper? Reflections of the mainmast when we're
shipping ten-foot seas cause visual whiplash—
much as they've been swallowing shadowed mountains
that stagger hugger-mugger down the screen.

Anyone can see your heels would rather
be kicked up, your elbows have more room.
Yells start exploding at Prometheus,
who just now ran out on the Olympics,
windblown flagrant torch aloft in his left hand.
Only steel nerves could dodge a draft like that,

and look where it got him. The gavel's falling,
but someone not me will have to hoist it up again.

Mickle Street
I'm queer for nouns or verbs that end in *–ickle*,
For bouncy trampolines, for trust and bluff.
We're told by those downtown that La Morbid's dull
Renouncing didn't rustle up enough
Bling to dazzle more than a few of them.
Turn on a dime, a channel. Those we flip
Ring truer than the frilly stratagem
Fern bars used to unfurl, and we know zip
About karate or brass knucks. To battle
The meltdown blues, lay out your Cups and Swords.
Don't doubt the Duke will hop down from the saddle,
His belt slung low. Check out the story boards:
Next year he trades his roan for a motorcycle.

MTC Cronin
Australia

THEGUNFIELD
The gun field shot anybody who walked on it. Of course the mountains
soon became snipers and the valleys the kinds of trenches that living
things cower in. This is what happens when you think the environment's
solely responsible.

HISLIFE
He was in possession of a functioning improvised device. His life. Brand
new stock or slightly damaged it was his life. It was a coronary colour and
certainly able to die of something. Most of the time he just let it whir
along in the corner but if he thought about outcomes he would alternate
the ending. Tomorrow it would be well lived. And the tomorrow after that
it would have been worth living.

THEHUMLESSHUMMINGBIRD
Outside my bedroom window is a bush. The bush makes no sound and

does not wake me. Inside the bush is more bush. I dream that inside the man there is more man.

THEOFFICEOFMYHAPPINESS

I lock the door of my office. The office of my happiness. Sometimes I lock the door when I am in it. Sometimes when I am out of it. The door, I have noticed, has a sticky lock.

Craig Czury
United States

Postmark Argentina—Buenos Aires, 1994

At the end of the table an explosion of love-making breaks out. Borges pounds his fist. Gardel tosses water in his face. Martin Fierro flashes a blade and slices his tie. This is a regular Monday night reading the future from the psalms of our hands. Gypsy scarves leaping from our mouths. Your little sister strikes up the harmonica, a tune heard so long ago the table cloth catches fire. Pablo's humongous breasts bleed against our wrists for us to drink. Geronimo! The waiter is now fifteen Janus faces on the backs of our chairs. Your mother walks in past her bedtime selling rose stems the women bite into snakes. Ah, the women with their intoxicated feet on the switch. A meaty strand of black hair writhes across the napkins. This music inside a plate of bones. You could reach through the tiles and lift out this night painted inside a burlap sack. In half an hour the nurse will bring you your bottle of wine. Let me kiss you now with that look on your face.

Postcards From Oregon—Newport, 1981

This is the picture postcard from sepia: the ocean belly-up between its sandy sheets and that beautiful sky last year with gulls so south now only a massive rusty hole. This is vintage saltfog laced with squid. The cliff house shadows a slow-burnt canvas fire. No one wishes you were here. This is as far as you can see our last steamer smoking the horizon. A torrential anguish biting a torrential blood wind. This is our old brown ghost looking back through the film.

One of us is a gargantuan tattoo you'd mistake for skin, another is a stuffed elk pecker hung with feathers to the floor. Someone else is a woman's bust laced with anchor rope. Everyone is grimy hair. I'm teeth like scales in a bucket of cod. The pool table's a sloppy drunk and the balls are stolid & smacked-around striped oranges. Today is Wednesday in the a.m. before 7. We all drink this briny java and careen off the bar until beer makes us healthy. Then someone else is a gargantuan tattoo, etc. At the Bay Haven—celebrating the holiday we call waking up.

Click!

The photographer's hunched over his camera screaming, That's it! The same moment Big Nana shifts to her champion bowling pose Miklós Radnóti is being exhumed from a mass grave, blood mixed with mud was drying in my ear, his last poem I'm reading in the bulb flash, blood-crusted from his overcoat pocket. Underdeveloped glimpse of Anna Akhmatova staring out of the torpor common to all of us in those days, faint smile of the woman who gave birth to me, her lips blue from the cold. That was a time when the dead could smile. My old man exhales a plume of cigar smoke, the afternoon is all fallen plaster, black stones, dry thorns. The afternoon has a difficult color made up of old footsteps halted in mid-stride. Yannis Ritsos coughs up a glob of tubercular phlegm. That's me, second to the left, spiking my flat-top with the palm of my hand, squeezed between Kafka and Calvino, who prop me up between sense and direction. Of course I'm late for school. Everything I need and reach for as I'm racing for the door breaks off in my hands. When I grab the door it doesn't open. It doesn't open, and I wake up running through the neighbors' yards where women are hanging sheets on clotheslines I brush, tangle, and, pumping my arms, lift myself off the ground, up, clear of the clotheslines, clear of the power lines. I'm treading the air above a crowd of tiny people who are chasing me when I wake up standing in the wings of an auditorium being introduced as a very important person I don't recognize and I've grown a beard. Walking out across the stage I'm not wearing any clothes. The house is packed with everyone in a tux or a gown with hairdos, I walk behind the podium feeling protected as I begin to read from a sheet of paper all the words are mixed up and what comes out of my mouth is gibberish when I wake up peeing the bed I'm covered with seeds it's my birthday and I'm 50 years old all my friends are teenagers.

Antonio D'Alfonso
Canada

Standing Behind Death

Standing behind death a prankster adlibs. An aria from La Bohème by Puccini. May the gods pay no regard to him. Spicy red peppers hang in the sun. From East to West, it is all the same. In every eye, the green light of contentment. Pop open the champagne waiting at her feet. A wink is an elephant's lie. Memory flickering, memory fluttering. Who are we tonight on this rooftop, Mesmerized by Chinese fireworks,

Embracing our love for never?

Ponctual

Punctual as usual evening strides the bright hollow, stops, wheels on her heels, glares about, wilfully soils the lustrous sky with amethystine furrows. With thin delicate fingertips thrumming her slender unclad thighs, she struts the large dim sheen and then with black fingers pinches sun's nose, pummels his mangy flanks, finally fillips him out of sight. She smiles at her fine attire, brushes the lapel on which lies moon pinned, whose puffy cheeks she passionately licks. Snuggled between her breasts, content with their long black kisses, he sucks in the Milky Way; he laps and sups his earthbound reflection.

Lobster

Born with the hard shell on white grume and bulging appendages, the lobster inhales air nimbly, a child sucking at mother's breast. Its antennae are water satellites of allergens. Crystal-ball eyes foretell prehistoric remains. Lob bathes – to quote Plato – in ocean's beauty and doesn't know it. On five pairs of legs, fragile as cartilage, it crawls slyly, alertly, pincers nipping here and there, and is as fierce as scorpion stinging strangers. The common type slumbers in large groups beside bored sun-flaccid tourists. Its cousin, the determined Americanus, builds sand castles, convinced all is well and democratic.

Subhrasankar Das

India

Horoscope

This shit can tear the joints of neurons, but it didn't.
Being bankrupt, the day may collapse like globules of iron, but it didn't

Only the dismantled horoscope is sneaking under the fake
 almanac.
and the pen made of paper is bleeding ...

The Perfumist

Capturing the postures of a photographer
is also a way to unlock his epistemic perspectives

One such winter morning,
in a foggy suburb,
a stranger had an encounter with a home.
He transformed it into a house,
then..into a hole...then into a void.
But actually it was a human !
Hiding in the hood of a rickshaw
a perfumist captured this scene
and made it viral..

The stranger broke the wall.
The perfumist joined him .
Then came a politician, a police , a father, a brother…
All of them thrust their weird rats of lust
 into the void.

Here, the materials for making home
are lying around.
The owner is missing.
Even from the formless rooms of the house,
comes
the smell of burning.

Lawdenmarc Decamora
Philippines

Self-Portrait as Open Flesh of an Undetermined Panic
Most of the panic remains virginal in the backyard, mostly
  quince-colored, growing
like a flower sitting on an acre of phrases, mostly gerund,
  echoing
the voiced Gustav Klimt canvas that speculates on a mottled
  shadow.
The figure of it is the sharp side of human,
the freckled face of suspicion
entering the green steel fences of our house, near the grass
that beds the pain, the pity, the first person
with a complex set of subjunctive mood. At about ten in the
  morning,
before lunch is served, short of parenthetical immensities
about the recent case of a dog, the doomed offering beneath the
  orange sun,
the children surround the area
where there is a smell drawing a familiar incident.
It's a funny fruit torn from the sight's memorial Eden
recalling a life in the hay, once mistakenly
begging for bones, sometimes barking at the neighbor's
election campaign ads-plastered tree,
shaking out what's coming in less, drily unnameable.
However, in the interest of ungrammatical bodies writhing into a
  tiny talented form,
a secret snapping in, then momentarily a scintillant revelation:
the children should know
the fleshy ground entails to stain and swell the inside
that is the given pronoun, the only thing escaping existence
for a dead goat, now slurping reciprocally red,
to sink the unknowing world in the deadest drink of panic. And
  that a stranger
from out of nowhere, appears, to finally recognize the goat,
  mistaken for a dog,

as open flesh of an undetermined time and space, as syntax
the rain accidentally builds.

Thad DeVassie
United States

Ghost Bus
What do they know of death, the foot-tired and the weary with their
parcels, their itineraries? Then like a dawning, an epiphany, they start
inching away from curbsides, from shelter benches, becoming quick
converts to pedestrianism, believing there is another way and politely
waving to the reaper behind the wheel who won't stop until he reaches
capacity.

Everything is Random
When a thief pried his way into our home with the intent to pillage and
inflict harm, I didn't flinch. Instead I said, *follow me,* and we walked out
the back door, avoiding the neighbor's peering eyes and resulting gossip,
then made our way a half-dozen blocks to the corner mini-mart. With the
exception of our awkward dance projected on a grainy, closed-circuit
security monitor, we moved undetected as we passed the Slushie machine
and overcooked roller food, until we could spot bounties of promise: A
deck of playing cards. Lock de-icer and Duralogs. Sudoku and disposable
razors. Beef jerky and more beef jerky. The stuff of impulse and biding
one's time, of uncommon necessity and banal utility in the dark hours
damn near close to this one. How it all found its way into four prized
aisles of a near-vacant mini-mart awash in fluorescent lighting remains a
distant supply chain secret, as perplexing as the novice cat burglar who,
without his stocking cap and nude panty hose screening his face, is just
another domesticated animal looking to make it through the day.

John Digby

United States

She Tells Me

She tells me that her flesh is
Inhabited by thousands of birds
I remove the rivers from her
The soft sleeve of sleep

    And discover
    Twin mountains of blood
    In which dolphins suddenly
    Flash into the sunlight

She is a child born too soon too late
Time that has lost its passage
A secret gathered from the language of birds
Her hair ripe with the games of sunlight

    Now I can imagine her
    She turns to song to blood to stone
    Circling this world
    A flame passing through the earth's shadow

Daughter of Lightning

She steps out of her head
with a necklace of kisses
wound around her throat
and her hair as brilliant
as a village burning
where she walks singing
among the flames
spreading terror
she takes one step forward
and causes whole cities
to take wing
whirling like a flock

of startled birds
she takes a step backwards
and the forests sleeping
between her breasts
shudder with sudden snowfalls
she opens her breasts
and shows you her heart
a ball of dancing flames
she opens her eyes
and shows you
two fathomless seas
in which she stands
directing a parade
of dead through your sleep
she opens her hands
and shows you
cities decaying among
the ribs of distant stars
she opens your eyes
with a kiss of electricity
mingled with pain
and the scent of roses
and beheads you in your sleep

As She Was Combing Her Hair

She was strolling past
combing her hair
and the lightning suddenly stretched its muscles
and clapped its hands
then the furniture in my room
began to shudder and sneeze
and everything burst into life
the roof blew off
and dolphins appeared sporting among the clouds
leaping through the smoke rings the sun was blowing
the roses on the wallpaper began singing
they opened their mouths

like tiny fledglings
and musical notes shaped like bubbles
streamed out the open window
everything in the room began to dance
my books my table my small lamp
and my pen too
writing its own wild automatic poem
everything was dancing with joy
I peered out of the window
and saw the sun following her
softly humming to itself
I rushed downstairs
and out into the street
to stop her and drag her back
into the crazy room
but she had simply disappeared

Mark DuCharme
United States

They Dream
after Ashbery

They dream only of what was
Pillorying exactly the least essential
The most abortive thing to be stockpiled
In the catalogue of honorific forms

They dream only of lesions grown in the throat
As if one had swallowed a Braille iteration
Of *The Epic of Gilgamesh* with notes for Hungarian speakers
None of whom dream wickedness in Italian

They dream only of the hallowed
The bumpy & heuristically forlorn
Even as they dream of wearing gabardine suits

& Scaling flashily the girders of the Zilwaukee Bridge

Which tremble with new awareness every time we touch them
As we drink lemonade & lurch at the ballyhoo
Of my & everybody's ramshackle façade
Toward which we dream rampant, ancient speakers, stereo or
        otherwise

Though we are poor, & our own dreams are often of the dead, or
        nearly dying
Who refurbish America with their long-lost cries, their ancient
        selves
Which cannot be heard, although the dead are already here
Faint as a manuscript of bones, until the trees go missing

Stammer
My immunity to Rilke makes neon obligatory
To standoffish weird sisters rocking
Though the hoops are foreign with trade school regalia
& I come to fidget, not to dither

When I carpool at all, which is all bound up in
The homonyms for tone arms which make me skittish
As registered plaster
Though I'll not likely be back here until sundown

When the balalaikas are returned to the parking garages
& We stammer like schoolboys who've just dissected a bug
In realtime amphitheaters of the starkness that harkens
To our betweens. But who are we anyway?

Perhaps ancient shadows on a modern joyride
Or perhaps just some replica of the hills that were starting to
        mean
Home to insomniacs when we can't look back
Or spill our guts in an emergency, remembering what we've
        become

95

Alison Dunhill
United Kingdom

Fragments
In the night's walls,
caterpillars of memory.

In the crowd,
the man's egg-head apple blossom.

On the journey,
blackthorn-straggled, cow parsley-clouded, larch-dangled hedge.

In their passages,
nerves flicker, resurrected light bulbs.
On the river,
a wasp's wreath lost in green.

Over hope's wide lake,
a bridge of energy.

Under the rust heads of sorrel,
a throbbing toad.

In the uncut barley field,
red tractors, yellow combines.

On the high sea barrier, over the salt marsh,
Giacometti sculptures.

In the refrigerator,
pink cartons of discovery.

On the backs of sheep, in evening sun,
stripes of milk.

Along the arterial road,
Hoovers of despair.

You Make Me Feel Brand New

And what if an entirely new sensation struck
at each intercontinental railway station;

glittered and fast-flickered my wrist veins,
my femur and my pancreas,

splattered my aortic valve,
splintered my cranium,

dispersed my shoulder blades in bougainvillea fragments
over Bologna's beautiful Alidosi bridge? Would I still rear

as your thrown lassoes perfectly gird me?
Then you stand on the filigree balustrade of Verona

surrounded by lotus flowers, lotus flowers.

I have thrust and wriggled out of my old form
and left its skin mottled and crisp

in wet snake grass.
I am new, forms welded, muscles toned.

You gaze down at me from the precipice.
I shine you the thousand lights of the Zürich See.

Alan Elyshevitz
United States

Insomnia, Part IX

I have mastered the elongation of time.
Horizontal is my orientation, my verbatim.
You think you are walking in bed
wearing a bad prescription. You cannot
awaken from arrhythmia nor sleep

97

through assembled fears. Sheep
have been my ridiculous emblem,
but these days you count only grandchildren.
I invite you to consider the marsupial
in which the young sleep soundly.
How many centuries since your ancestors
set fire to their rest and chartered
newfound light to last until dawn?
I was there in the space between baobabs,
dressed in infallible nostrils and teeth,
there to witness the fumigation
of grievances against your own nature.
Your torment is the retroactive hours
of Prudhoe Bay or Tierra del Fuego.
In between, on Route 40 West,
you bisect the lackadaisical scenery:
longhorn steer or long red mesa.
This highway was built for wide states,
for you to contemplate inopportune
vegetation tangled in your thoughts.
I flatten the view to your prognosis:
California! Every night I hear you
banging that wall you call the sea.

John Ennis
Ireland

Snow Ploughing

> *la vida es sueño y los sueños sueños son,*
> *– Pedro Calderón de la Barca*

I wake to a white championship of snow
and cursed be the sweaty soul who fails to plough
in a straight line, but some sneak stole my moulding board.
Search as I will for it for chest-torn hours in blizzard
swept desert warehouses, where they keep ploughshares,

not a sign of it. Just what some of my neighbours
will do to you to win the senior championship
before the thaw. Then, ahead of myself, of faith, a leap
God wrestle as might to fix it on,
the indubitable board, --just got a used one on Amazon –
despair. I'm ploughing nowhere fast, as Alison Balsom
sounds her trumpet voluntary, dream times's over. Alas,
too much indeed I do presume, my last presumption
pure soul bouncing on the bosom of Alison Balsom.

Termite Vomitorium
The vomitorium these days is empty
padlocked for the great and mighty
are still offshore in pleasure crafts
domained with oaks at their backs,
even if the afternoons are green tea.
Termites of this termite time all agree
the hulks that crush are full of pity,
so, complain a little, hum and haw,
fall silent again beneath the status quo
whose wealth is not that measurable.
Come, a termite to chew the padlock, enable
the unwashed to troop in with full breasts
vomit what lies on them of elites, their guests
pray typhoons to share out treasure chests.

Elaine Equi
United States

Recurring Dog
In the first dream, the dog is disguised as a cat.

In the second dream, when I pet him, the dog turns into
        chocolate.

In the third dream, the dog is a ball of dirty yarn which I scoop
        up

and lay over my chest to muffle the sound of my rapidly beating heart.

Recently, I was surprised to discover that the idea of "care
      animals"
has caught on even in the dream world. Apparently, these
      nocturnal
service animals have been trained by totem-leaders in the collective
unconscious, to gently nuzzle sleepers who show signs – tossing,
turning, twitching, grinding – of experiencing particularly
      gruesome
or humiliating nightmares. But they do it with sweetness and
      finesse,
so the person isn't forced to wake abruptly -- instead is gradually
      led
on an invisible leash to explore more pleasant terrains before
      morning.

Uncollected
My poem with the blank stare and secret smirk.
My poem with the mojo of a thousand emojis.
My poem like a tame ocean.
My anorexic poem sucking for days on a single syllable.
My hearty midwestern potluck poem.
My poem with the heady air of an Alpine inn.
My poem that still suffers in the twenty-first century from
      neurasthenia.
My city poem with its chorus of paper-skyscraper-dolls.
My lace-edged unromanticism.
My poem that likes talking to strangers.
My pathetic poem.
My homeopathic poem.
My glow-in-the-dark poem.
My poem that is finished by elves.

Gradually, Gills
merge
      emerging

into the antediluvian
bloodstream.

Transposed
air is water;

water,
     air —

a busy, frizzy
bringing and brought
behind the somehow seductive
fanfare of fins.

O for a menial task
to preoccupy me
while the big picture
resolves itself

and evolution completes
its long day.

It's like being inside
a rainy aquarium

or the watershed
of a giant teardrop.

Dry water,
     liquid land.

Poems are paperweights,

ballast to keep our words
from floating away.

R. G. Evans
United States

All Newborn Gods
All newborn gods
are anonymous as birdsong.
They speak the same language
of need, dance the same mazurka
in cradle, crib, or creche.
All newborn gods bestow
blessings of shit and piss
unto a world that doesn't know
it needs changing as well.
The parents of all newborn gods
are as stunned as virgins
visited by angels who scream
hosannas in the middle of the night
while the unblessed world sanely sleeps.
All newborn gods
could eat the sun and moon,
the earth and all the sky,
would devour their own tails
if it weren't for the swaddling clothes.
Over the heads of all newborn gods
stars cluster like berries. Pick one.
It's as good as any other:
the light where all begins.

Yellow Poem, Blue Poem, Red Poem
Yellow poem says it's sorry
that everything passes away.
Sunset. Oak leaves in fall--
you know, the things poets say

102

when they mean they are afraid.
Yellow poem says go on,
be afraid. Be yellow.
If you never write a poem again,
at least you'll still have fear.

Blue poem says come on and
have a drink. It knows twelve bars
where you can sink good and deep
down in the blue. It says
the sky ain't cryin', baby.
That's just words to take the place
of a scream that would come out blue.
Blue poem says now drink. Now smoke.
Come be the whole blue goddam sky.
Red poem don't say nothing.
Red poem is a rope with one knot
in your chest, one knot in your throat,
one knot right between your eyes.
Red poem knows you know
it's the one true poem.
It's in your blood. It's in your eyes.
It's the color your words make
when you ain't got time
for no more yellow or blue.
Red poem's the one with teeth.
Red poem's got you by the balls.

Zoë Fay-Stindt
United States

Her Beak Inside Me
While the heron works on me, I sleep,
dreaming of a small fire struck in my womb,
a coiled army of ants caught in some dark recess
of my throat. She takes every bone out

103

to clean, boiling each, drying them out
on the bank. I worry she'll mistake
a bent piece of driftwood for my clavicle,
subbing in a crab's abandoned shell
where the parietal bone should fit.

Others gather while she works:
the red squirrels pick at felled pecans,
the street beagles pant uneasily.
My mother's in the house
washing pots over and over,
something she can't rub clean
sticking to their sides. A sparrow has just
flown into his reflection, now stumbling,
nauseously, around our rotting porch.

In this house as old as us, things are splintering.
Mom flicks tree frogs off the window screen
for each fissure: her brother's ailing body,
flick, her father's sickness resurfacing, *flick*,
each lost friend clicking offline, *flick, flick, flick.*
Underneath the window, the dog collects their bodies
from the grass, drops them from his soft lips
onto beds of magnolia sheddings, the wide, glossy leaves,
the wilted petals, their tough seeds. Each pale belly
still thumping, their greens starting to dull.

I wait for the shore to reappear,
for the tide to go out, for the heron
to withdraw her long beak. When she's finished,
she'll sew me up with willow thread, send me
to the water. I'll pull all the clams up
by their knife-tops, try to boil them clean,
the water cloudy with river mud, stinking of swamp.

Scott Ferry
United States

shame dream
my clothes still off and my skin blistering
in front of the windows i see a line of people
i didn't notice before reflected in the periphery
and when i turn my head to focus on them
they turn into rosemary and lilac

they turn into statues of horses
i can't find my clothes and now my skin
is peeling off in continents and the bluebone
silk of my real skin glows when the dead layers
are wiped away

my penis is sapphire and my nipples are tangerine
and my hair is pearl and my fingers grow into vines
with winged flowers springing from the knuckles
the people are gone but i simmer in
coiled wait

when i wake i am ashamed i have shown too much
i am ashamed that my underskin surges out
like a swarm i am ashamed that these multipleasures
bound inside my pulses i am ashamed to appear
too much like a god

tea and the taste of dusty paper
the spirits of my relatives always wear
ashen stove top hats

when they usher into my half-sleep
like a melted pantomime

they seem to be exhaling chamomile
100 years left on the breath

they seem to feel welcome as i try to focus

on their eyes but the eyes

of the dead look into every doorway
at once so the lids trap time

their mouths speak every word
through a blur-sand maw

so all i hear is weeping and backwards
shouting and oily songs

but they never consider me
the caretaker of this theater

just a man somewhere up in the rafters
who thinks he controls the stage

pulling ropes lifting props making a glittery
wooden moon float as if by magic
and they turn through the walls regardless
of whether i draw the curtain of sleep

around all of these lost voices around
all of these mute seats

these ticket stubs
in my teeth

S.C. Flynn
Ireland

Progress Report
It was raining indoors when I woke today
to the heavy drops spattering my pillow.
While I drank my first coffee at eleven
a rainbow hung between the stove and fridge
and the dark clouds retreated to the corners.
The voice began to speak about midday,

saying this was another phase of life,
that everyone is a work of art
but originality is another matter,
not to break the law until it breaks you first
and that I shouldn't expect to understand
until I receive the call. The objects around me
contain a fraction of the answer, I'm sure,
but they stay silent as the rain returns.

Jester

The sober heart of a laughing multitude,
I still worship the broken statues where they lie
buried in the mud, and then with my dirty feet
trample proud carpets. My hat is a hydra,
each point a spear of contempt that sprouts
two more when cut off, but there will be no fire
to heal their bleeding stumps. I plant in that same mud
a stick mounted with a pig's bladder
and they laugh; if I planted a sword,
they would bow down before it. It is always me
the other nine turn on, when the order
for decimation is given; me, the tenth in line,
the sober heart of a laughing multitude.

Jack Foley
United States

Love Song

I miss you like the bowl of oatmeal left out in the rain and eaten
        by wolves.
I miss you like the angel who missed the diamond-studded pole
        in the middle of downtown Dallas.
I miss you like the yellow-tailed bird in the outskirts of Detroit.
I miss you like the disease of overeating.
I miss you like the baseball of malnutrition misses the bat of
        individuality.
I miss you like the fallen angel risen up only to discover that he
        is tangled in the barbed

wire of a Minneapolis telephone line.

I miss you like the penis of downtown Los Angeles.

I miss you like the statue of the Virgin Mary defaced by vandals
in Mer-St.-Jean.

I miss you like the ocean of Guadalupe and the sea of Carmen
Miranda.

I miss you like the deaf uncle of a Samothrace in over-populous
Pebble Beach.

I miss you like the Catholic priest secretly wearing a bikini
under his bicycle pumps.

I miss you like the mother of Martin Scorsese as she tells him
that he is in fact Armenian.

I miss you like mumps and mumble-de-peg.

I miss you like snowbush and sneezewort.

I miss you like snatch block (which is "a fairlead having the
form of a block that can be opened to receive the bight
of a rope at any point along its length")

I miss you like the mountains of Fresno and the clouds of Aix-la-
Chapelle as they extend a welcoming hand to Christ the
Redeemer, who has decided to move to California.

I miss you like the Virgins who haunt the telephone wires in
which the angel, discouraged, has fallen into troubled sleep.

I miss you like troubled sleep.

The Prophet
      —after Zukofsky

bridges flame mystery far megalith
mahabharata stone *birth-child* melos lone
twinned twined heavy auspicious bright
indian *in dios* lost regained
valum votan pebbles sand grain
brush canvas *fallacy* time lips
beauty failing open heaven *fall*
.

rainbow rainbow rainbow ash wind

for José Argüelles (1939-2011)

108

Garcia Lorca
murders the dove
with an eraser of gold.
he holds open the door
so the wind can kiss the cheeks
of The Sisters of Mercy.
he bows to the fathers
with an empty violin.
on the tattered stoop he watches
as the children play
ring-a-rosy
and defends the sparrows
on the rooftops of Spain.
he turns to me
with his marvelous eyes.
he turns to me
his marvelous eyes.

Noir
She stared at me the way an empty tin can stares at a cooked
          peach.

She was wearing black panties and no bra.

She said "No" to me in Chinese. I didn't understand Chinese.

She looked at me the way a Hottentot looks at a missionary. A
          hot Hottentot.

If she had any more curves she would have been an illegal pitch.

She said, "How long have you been around?" I said, "Long enough to
know trouble when I see it." She said, "Trouble—how do you spell that?"
I said, "T-h-a-t."

The revolver was still hot in her hand. Her husband lay dead at her feet. "I
didn't do it," she said. I believed her.

"How long had your husband been in a wheel chair?" I inquired. "Since a few hours after our wedding night." "He couldn't move any more?" "He didn't move then."

She said, "My name's Virtue." I said, "I knew your sister, Prudence." She said, "How many times a week?"

She said, "I usually take a book to bed. But when I don't have a book, I have to make do with what I've got. You like red pajamas?"
She said, "You wanna know how to make a film noir? Turn off
        the lights."

(long pause)

I turned off the lights.

When she took off her clothes she was a violent red bird with a
        beak of gold.

Linda Nemec Foster
United States

The Hunchback on Isola Madre, Italy
His back is bent and stuffed into a thin blue jacket with a broken zipper. He doesn't say a word, but has a chronic cough. The younger man in the orange shirt that accompanies him is curt and gruff. Yells at him to "andiamo" and, otherwise, ignores him. When the hunchback reaches the stunning botanical gardens surrounding the Villa de Borromeo, he sits on a bench and smokes. Doesn't pay attention to the red azaleas, the rhododendrons, the wall of camellias and its cascade of pale faces. Not even the huge Kashmir Cypress, the largest in Europe, gets a glance. Halfway through his cigarette, a white peacock approaches him, and with a shrill cry, spreads its glorious plumage. He's tempted to blow gray smoke into that cloud of feathers and see how the peacock reacts. With surprise, with anger? Would the cloud disappear into the early evening sky? Before he can find out, his young companion starts to complain about catching the last ferry back to Stressa, the smoldering cigarette, the hunchback's annoying habit. The roots of the giant cypress hear the

110

coughing as the tree's Oriental needles fall like rain in the gravel courtyard.

Stadtpark, Graz

Early March and the hyacinth are already in bloom. Vibrant yellow and muted lavender surround the overbearing fountain—a gift from Vienna in 1873. Loud derelicts—drunk on cheap beer and themselves—chase stray dogs and each other. A Buddhist monk discretely appears from nowhere and takes a sequence of photos with his iPhone: a bare cypress, red graffiti on a cement wall, two Pomeranians digging in the dirt. He is wrapped in an orange robe with gold trim. For him, there is no where but here. This windy day in southern Austria where the drunken man with purple hair sings a dirge filled with love. Or lost love. Or almost love. Or never love. Like this neverland nestled in a map near the Slovene border. Maybe the monk asks the quiet sycamore, "Where am I going?" Its branches filled with no clouds and a pale blue. He spends an hour waiting for an answer. Anybody's guess, he guesses. And the answer would be totally right and totally wrong, depending on where you are at any given moment. Meanwhile, the shadows of the dogs and the drunks collide.

Dede Fox
United States

The Golem Moves to Cut-n-Shoot
Enough of that frigid attic,
Prague's brutal winters
that last hundreds of years.
No more fringed rabbis chanting
Cabalistic prayers for my creation,
demanding my protection against Blood
Libel, lies of the ignorant or evil
determined to pursue their own agendas.

A rabbi created me, left me voiceless,
cruel irony for one with *EMET*: Truth
etched across a clay forehead.
His G-d never breathed a soul into me,

111

yet he demanded my blind obedience,
called *me* a monster for my violence,
repented for his mis-conception, and
killed me by wiping out a single Hebrew letter.
EMET transformed to MET, my "death."

I was never loved.
Rage brought me back to life.
I escaped while Jews prayed;
Shabbat means nothing to the soulless.
I joined a security force,
exchanged my inhumanity for passage to Texas.
where I covered my tattoo with a cowboy hat,
joined the Aryan Brotherhood,
became one of many clay men with empty eyes
who believe truth lies in their tattoos.

Jeff Friedman
United States

Hole in My Head

There's a hole in my head the size of a half dollar—and who knows how
deep? The surgeon advised me to leave the wound open, because, she
said, it would heal faster, but it's already been two years. When I go out,
birds plunge at my bright dome. I swing my arms to keep them away, but
some still land and dip their beaks into the hole as if searching for insects
or worms. Something must scare them because they take off quickly. I
clean out the hole with a damp piece of cloth and find leaves, stray hairs,
pebbles, coins, blessings and aphorisms. For a while I wore a large
bandage over the hole, but then my head would swell as if it were filling
up with fluid. When I'd slowly remove the bandage, thoughts shot out and
showered through the air like glitter. Always, a few broken thoughts
would be stuck to the bandage. Each day, I stare into the mirror and hold
a mirror over my head to get a good look inside the hole. I see some
creature deep below, turning over to show its orange belly, and numerous
clichés bobbing near the surface. When I shift the mirror, my head
disappears, and only the hole remains.

Catching the Monster

On Main Street, I spot the monster in the crowd. He's clean shaven, but there are red nicks on his cheeks and chin. He's got long claws that can rip a chest apart in seconds. No one in the crowd appears to notice that the monster is among them. I follow closely weaving in and out until I'm almost stepping on his heels. Suddenly he turns to face me. "You're a monster," I say. He licks the stain of blood from his lips. "Is that so bad?" he asks. "There are many missing," I answer "and bones scattered throughout the city." Without even a glance, people walk by or around us. Neon signs blink. Cars jam the noisy streets growing jumpy, music blasting from open windows. "There are always many missing, always trails of clues leading everywhere and nowhere," he says. I grip his forearm, causing him to grimace. "I'm taking you in." The monster breathes in my face. His breath is sweet as if he has eaten a sweet meat. He stares deep into my eyes, searching for my secrets. "If you believe in monsters, perhaps you are a monster," he says. "Isn't that what all monsters say?" I ask. "Point well taken," he answers, "but you do have a powerful jaw, yellow eyes and spotted skin—like the rest of us monsters." I cuff his wrist to mine, head to the station to turn us both in—for the reward.

Bear Fight

When Liza fell in with the bear, I was more than disappointed as I had been in love with her since childhood. "What's he got that I don't?" I asked as we walked past the diner together. "He's a bear." She let go of my hand. "He gets a little jealous when I'm out with my friends." "Why do you want to be with a bear anyway?" Two teenagers pushed past us with their skateboards. Balloon floated above Main Street, announcing a sale at the furniture shop. "Why do you want to be with me?" she asked. We parted ways when the light changed, but later I went to her home dressed as a bear. She opened the door. "Come in," she said, putting her arms around me. "You don't smell like a bear," she said, Then in walked the bear, with a fierce look on his face. He growled and so did I. He cuffed me, so I cuffed him back. Then we grappled with each other, bear hugging until Liza stepped in between us and held out her hands. "I'm sick of bears," she said. "Get out of here." I ripped off my bear mask. "I'm not a bear," I said. The bear ripped off his. "I quit this game," he said. "I'm not a bear either." Liza removed her mask, and she wasn't Liza.

113

We ran away as fast as we could. I made it back to my place and locked the door, turning on the outside light, but all night I heard her huffing.

Joanna Fuhrman
United States

The Algorithm Ate My Lunch
I wanted everyone to feel the way my teeth vibrated, but when I posted my glow-in-the-dark selfie only the closet mermaids noticed. I didn't blame anyone. I knew the oceans were walking heavy-footed on the land. It was one of those afternoons when I was sure that God was the series of tubes connecting my brain to the torso of a deer. Was it possible that the self was larger than the country that birthed it? Could a mouth open large enough to accommodate the girth of a bloated nation's whale? I hung a sign that read "hope" on the taxidermized body of an owl and waited for applause. Children gathered around to worship, sticking microchips and slivers of sunlight in its missing, blinking eye.

My American Name is Money
A ghost wears a white sheet for Halloween, haunts the hallways of the dismantled university Beneath the floorboards, the rich keep their family secrets in coffins shaped like closed eyes. Behind the chalk board, language dissolves. A lawn gnome comes to life and falls in love with the space inside a wondering zero.

In the basement, soldiers posing as statues photocopy pictures of a scholar's missing torso. The faculty bathroom overflows with grad student tears.

I would like to tell you that this poem is a water gun shooting truth into the eyes of the oblivious chancellors, that language is a net ready to catch the falling bodies of uninsured adjuncts, but I know that didacticism is the enemy of poetry, so instead I offer you a blank stare. No, it's more of a gaseous cloud, loose molecules disguised as a body of prose.

The Matrix
I was not surprised to learn that character of Smurfette in *The Matrix* was played by the Holy Trinity: her brain was God, her body Jesus, her

weapons holy ghosts. The actual Smurfette is angry that in real life she never got to kick any digital asses. I tried to explain to her that in the current version of 51st wave feminism, we hate violence, but her hands have already turned into boxing gloves. Despite my pleas, she swings them wildly into the binary code mustache of Burt Reynolds.

When I wake up, my mouth has been replaced with a centipede that crawls across the screen of my face. My husband has been replaced by a young Keanu Reeves who looks like he's remembering the thrill he felt when he first wrote his name in pee.

In my chest, a television is playing the movie's commercial break: an ad for imitation pheromones, staring the ghost of Ronald Reagan.

In the tunnels of the ad, those spaces between the pixels, a version of myself is dressed as a female Orpheus. Like always, I'm stuck looking back at that moment again, perceiving both the lighting flash of the future and the dark everything of the past.

In The Matrix Starring Nicolas Cage

Neo is a piss-ass drunk, and it doesn't matter if alcohol is only an idea. Meaning detaches from language and flies in slow motion like shampoo commercial hair. The absent women shift behind the curtains, a mother's face camouflaged by a William Morris floral, a sister's breath hidden by the smell of an off-season fireplace. The 21st century is riding a bloodshot Ferrari into the mouth of climate change, and it needs pure vodka to make it okay. Nic is naked all the time. Even naked, he sweats through his clothes. Even when he's fully dressed his dick swings unsheathed. You try lassoing the sky's panopticon with only a goddamned body part. He knows the world isn't real, so why not just buy a big-ass blowup doll? Why not just wear your rubber Donald Trump mask to crowded theatre and flail your octopi limbs at the screen?

C.M. Gigliotti
Germany

Rigor (Amor)tis

She cleaves the obscene laminated tapestries from the walls. She listens to songs that do her triumphing for her. She does her own weeping, enough for a river, which she rafts on the board of a ribcage wracked with sobs. She strangles the notes that escape her vocal cords in the dark. She prays, prostrate, and waits reply. She peels the flesh from her fingertips.

She runs.

She cleans the cavity of her chest, seals the letters with wax, buries them in a box. She follows the voices, farther pff than ever. She showers, long enough to forget what she was thinking of. She lets aisles and meals slip by. She slips off her dress, off her raft, drowns in the pages of books. She lulls herself to sleep with the soundtrack of the city she left behind. She writes new letters to old friends. She hangs her clothes, her hopes, anything but herself. She keeps silence for the voices that answer her. She bandages her fingers.

Five Years
the car
your father
Saturday night
pea coat snug

34th and Macy's
and the block of dreams
                    (nightmares
                    a few blocks north)

extra-
ordinary
to the last

you call yourself a citizen
                    (emphasis on city)
because you came with a price on your head
in the days before you spoke
and it set you free

                    (but perhaps you're fooling yourself
                    like when you claim
                    your pen can touch immortal)

February is a spiteful chill

                    (dares your passion to keep you warm)

listening to a singer
wonder what will happen
in the last five years

you come not from afar
and you see
beyond the window
                    palms against glass
                    loving too the shiver the sting

that five city years
are the only five years
                    (even if it turns you wispy as a spring wind)
the car
                vessel of solitude
                city unbounded
the lights
                reflect the city celestial
the music
                (even cities must have an end)
and you too

Daniela Gioseffi
United States

The Lily Pad
        Morning:
She pulls a French horn from the bodice of her dress,
tries to play it.
No sound comes out.
She begins to weep
but the cries she makes
sound like a horn played
far off in the distance.

117

Noon:

She puts the French horn back into the bodice of her
    dress,
runs to the river,
leaps in,
the weight of the horn
carries her to the bottom.
The same water fills her ears
that flows through the horn.
She hears its sound
sighing in her head.

    Night:

She swims to the surface dragging the French horn
    with her.
Her hair has turned white.
She drowns with the horn clutched to her shriveling
    lips.
Her white hair floats out all around her:
Now she is a lily pad
with a frog
singing on her breast.

Chrissie Gittins
United Kingdom

Velcro

We gave the same name to a rat
as we did to a giraffe,
a daisy was also a rhododendron.
When we pulled a lemon drizzle cake
out of the oven we called it bara brith.

People walked up and down the street
calling out to their neighbours –
'Dave', Lulu', 'Marissa'.
It was Frank, Lalia and Shannon
who called back.

Driving was treacherous.
A sign for South Wales also said Honolulu.
The motorways were strewn
with cars in the middle of u-turns.

'We don't speak your language,'
said the tea-cups.
'We don't understand your implication,'
we replied.

The police put up cordons
and danced in the spaces between.
From the cellophane on the bandstand
drifted the words 'beautiful', 'comfort', 'never'.
That was when the tide turned.
Each word aligned with its meaning
and stayed there,
anchored and hooked like leather to Velcro.

Ray Gonzalez
United States

Las Ramas

I began to listen inside the stanza of a poem and heard individual sounds
as *gripa* or *airlo* or *ar* calling to each other. A *gripa* is a creature that
cries out, an *airlo* a floating wing. I don't know what an *ar* might be,
though it tunes itself. What kind of union did these sounds proclaim?
Hearing these cries put me on the other side of the poem where growth
resides. I moved among forceful sounds in my first attempt at the poem.
What would happen if a *gripa* left the poet behind? Decisions about the
language would be based on the after-darkness following the encounter.
Radiant light between words fertilizes syllables around it. For length, I
chose eight lines, which permit a speaker to make his move. It was the
sound of my open mouth, *la rama* coming out, the word related to a
Spanish word for root. The notes that fell off *la ramas* allowed the
shadows in the poem to encircle the throat of the speaker, as in roots
spreading around a tree trunk, this situation changing constantly because
the more you add sound to the poem, new words appear on their own,

119

thus entering the text as the speaker pulls *las ramas* out of his chest before finishing the poem.

Blue Car

There is a theory that says when you drive the blue car into the sun, the other world will fill it with gasoline and you can get there without having to leave your vehicle. Study the previous sentence to find the road map. The spare tire in the trunk has nothing to do with universal consciousness and the steady skill of rebuilding it into a sleek and powerful engine to cross the stars. The steering wheel used to have the duty of combing God's hair. Bringing faith into this says you should be riding a bicycle instead. There is a theory that says when you turn around and drive it into the moon, you must have your license in hand because the craters never welcomes vehicles in reverse.

What if the driver wants to walk? The blue car was parked outside for several days and was broken into one night and the classic eight-track player was stolen, though no one could resell it because they didn't know what it was. There is a theory that commands an understanding of the choice of a blue car, model unknown, and how it influenced literary movements that kept the imagination running at full speed, the loneliness of this obvious to the pedestrian that refuses to get into the car when it pulls over and the driver says, "Get in."

Ten Objects

> *Lordosis—inward curvature of the spine*
> *Self-conquest—to overcome one's worst characteristics*
> *Genotype—the genetic constitution of an individual*
> *Belladonna—deadly nightshade*

Taking the belladonna affects the genotype, which prevents self-conquest but allows a severe case of lordosis to take place.

Picking the belladonna strains the lordosis and moves some DNA, thus redefining the geonotype without the brain considering self-conquest.

Overcoming the need for self-conquest cancels that day's search for belladonna, instigating a new strain that, once again, shifts the genotype and lessens the pain of lordosis.

The lordosis points the individual toward the earth, making it easier to pick the belladonna without the danger of upsetting the balance between the current genotype and the self-conquest in the background.

The genotype is not necessarily the driving force behind clearing the field of belladonna because the lordosis prevents such a sweeping and creates desire, thus bringing self-conquest back into the picture.

Self-conquest makes the belladonna grow at the borders of vision, moving the individual with the painful lordosis toward newer territory where the genotype has a clearer path to the healing sun.

The belladonna prefers darkness, so the genotype is twisted in an unexpected path that begins to heal the lordosis and leaves self-conquest up in the air.

Lordosis is a path given toward self-conquest when the genotype of belladonna is felt.

Genotypes are stored in the ribs, their invisible evolution forcing self-conquest that avoids lordosis after the consumption of belladonna.

The belladonna in the ground resembles a curved spine.

The Same Window
What should I say? That Nostradamus uttered in a strange tongue only known to him as he wrote down his prophecies? Perhaps I should mention the theory that peacocks are proud of their beautiful tails and feathers, but the peacock scream comes each time the bird looks down and sees its ugly, black foot. Even my father, writing in a gnomic book, told me that the bandit beheaded in his boyhood village was the man who ran away with my father's grandmother. What does this have to do with Amsterdam, San Francisco, or the brittle streets of El Paso? Where should I sweat next? Someone wrote that Columbus scribbled frantic notes on the margins of a manuscript by Marco Polo. If textbook heroes were part of my schoolboy fantasies, I won first place in a fourth-grade art contest by drawing the Nina, Pinta, and Santa Maria, swallowing my Texas education that said the magic aspect of life had to do with great discovery by three Spanish ships and my brown skin was simply an

121

evolutionary mistake—a hidden conquest of genes and DNA no talented fourth grader could conceive in his wildest crayon colored dreams. Yet, what was the year when I made my first cardboard electric guitar, taping an empty cigar box my father gave me onto a yardstick I stole from my mother, the teacher? The box was the body of the guitar and the ruler was the neck marked with precise frets where I rocked out and did air guitar to early Beatles. What should I sing next because a tune titled "Alligator Elevator" has been ringing in my head for days. I have not invented the lyrics because a dog crossed the street in search of the swimming reptile on the same day I thought of the title. I imagine the secrecy of elevators must be kept from the world because today, as I waited for the first winter snow, I saw beautiful Chinese silk being passed from hand to hand, the shoulders of the traders obscured in the tremendous flakes of white that erased further celebration and put me in a position to praise the details associated with a strange intelligence I found escaping through the window. This made me recall the day Lao-Tse told me he was carried in his mother's body for sixty-two years, and that is why his hair was white at birth.

The Wheels
The wheels on display, each thumb holy and not there, breath petals afraid and gasping as three hydrangeas grow out of control. Where is the momentum, the altars of conceit kneeling into their own shadows? Yearn for a fish bone and the first borne. Frequencies of squash and celery, a sipped omission falling down the stairs to dream again. The diseased cherry tree in the backyard weeps a sap from its bark for the first time. The tiger on display, a plastic starfish in your hair, one sandal petrified, half the rain cloud and the entire notebook. Night after night, the cyber enemy and a manifest Paradiso, blood on the toast and the wooden floor misunderstood. Crowds of computer children afraid to kiss and learn. The wheels on display, rain forests chest heavy with marked avenues and denied bowls of hot noodles. Must be the water wars and the dying tree fielding suggestions.

122

Patricia Goodrich

United States

After Picasso

Who abandons a feather duster in wanton disregard blue head silver ball a frame a woman who outlives herself the head white porcelain disconnected bronze holey pelvic bone who are you encased marrow broken fingertips oh juliet you can reach fingers tingle with phantom pain who are the bodies all in clay fired unfired glazed and plain who would cast the first glass whose breath lasts given shape by heat molten past ardor's cooling captured for eternity who sits under a gray canopy whose mind moves as abalone strings suspend their song as if today were any other who can say enough and look away

What time passes a sparrow seed strewn squirrel in the wings waiting for what will be what storm what brown leaf what company he keeps whatever screen divides always there is another side a coin flipped whatever the cost a penny nickel quarter dime loss of love or friend what friendship does allow odds or even more what enemy disavows the lie eyes feast on what's before the butchered pig the pigeon shot for what for perching on rafter thinking he's out of range what kind of man pulls the trigger what woman stands by side what iridescence in the death what spot of blood the pine boards hide what package wrapped casually in the blotting cloth

Where times consequence is no coincidence where child digs a hole for dog the road where death tracked him down the ground where earth received where tree shadows Sunday mornings where church empty rows and rows where tomorrow lies in possibility where water surges underground cutting stone where children climb king and queen side by side a mockery where pretend rules upside down somersault salute a stick where stem bends flesh where marks blood rises crumbs in pocket flea on fox where woman watches carcass stripped hop hop there are we

Why choose black when blue lay near who cares picasso andywarhol red mug franklloydwright nameless woman whose face a blind man cannot recognize ewe and lamb limestone white newyorkcity in a globe shadow figures who ride the metro no one looks out the window or meets another's eye how hard it is not to care blur the edges what focus it takes

123

no matter where who can move beyond the frame who moves beyond the
frame different questions entirely who thinks too much cannot answers
find one is not enough two too restricts makes choice inevitable who
looks for answers is the fool those who shape the questions rule

Ken Hada
United States

Making Love on Mars
I brought her here for romance.
After drinks, dinner and a short dance,
I take her hand and lead her to a place
undisturbed by the crowds.

We stroll through the gardens, feeling
the closeness only strangers know.
Her foot slips on a red rock
on the red-tattered path. The only path
we know to take. The only way
to Eden, where, on a bed of laurel leaves

I lay her head in the crook of my arm,
bend close for a kiss – our squinting eyes
protecting us from the red glare,
inviting us to certainty we left behind.

Dying on Mars
I never left. I thought I would, planned
to go more than once, but things kept me here.
I became fixated with red glow.

At the end of your days, your mind
looks backward but finds little to hold.
The empty bucket has betrayed

me. It can never be filled if the holes
cannot be patched. So, here I remained.

Made the best of it – enjoyed myself

fishing, watching birds, and making love.
What else would one want? My only
complaint – everything I see now

everything I have seen for years
is red. I know only red: fish, birds,
even my beloved lies red

before me in the rocky surface
I made a home, red in these strange
hills, where I hope, at last, someone

will dig a good grave for me,
and erect a white cross, unstained,
for a time, unsaturated by red.

Philip Hammial
Australia

Ex Cathedra
On location where trance folk snag –
a drum machine that scrolls down
to Swamp's End, sky stuff spilt
from the quaffing cup of a funeral lord. Might take years
to sort this mess, one sniveling ambush after another
slowing us down. Do we really
natives spot? – some people so populous, if only
they'd stop fibrillating & build beach bodies we might
have a better world: nine steps
to any distance, nine to any wish come true over terrain
as smooth as sex with an overweight transsexual
on April Fool's Day. Which, bugger, is today. If only
we'd checked our calendar before we left
for that raven-viewing party, those obnoxious
ornithologists with their bird calls that pulled the lame

out of their wheelchairs & sent them dancing
down the aisle for a blessing from a priestess
who insisted, & we quote: "Another inch
in this sealed room & the funeral will break
its only wheel."
                    That
was some experience, Candomblé by the feel of it, so
frenzied it makes us want to shout words like poets
with string habits, puppets to manipulate
as to brilliance we come by fits & starts.

Grand Theft Auto
Want to know how it happened?
I'll tell you how: a 3rd rail stoush
with a six-mule handicap, Hunky & Dory
sorting out their differences – who
nods when & if it's a sin to grin
at the great man's funeral. As expected
I say "Why not?" I say "It's time (while we're at it)
to sort the grannies, which die today & which
on Thursday next." Are you motivated
to conjure up a regret? I'm only asking because
the riding in these parts has been a bit too roughshod
for my liking (No, I don't share Teddy Roosevelt's
enthusiasm for). When we got to that beach we saw
that he'd made a right royal spill & wasn't prepared
to clean it up. Kinfolk curlicues & a making whoopie
scam – he left us no choice, we brought them to bear
& boy did he clean; you could have whistled
a dozen dogs home: sheer delight, let's sit tight
& watch the clouds roll in; forty days
& forty nights & they're still coming; maybe
we should finish carving that canoe; maybe
you could toss a few of those asylum pennies
our way; we're about to get all gussied up
& make our way to Golgotha; me & Garibaldi
if we get there whole the plan is to play
the local hoi polloi fast & loose, vamp
their plugs, spill their beans, with any luck

126

might even flog a few copies of my latest
The Petrochemical Songbook. "OK
everyone it's time to sing along" – Gall
upon gall, 50 miles of RCA!

Anger
Lots to be angry about: gunk
on our sheets & the fact that the merry-go-round,
jerked to a halt, is moving in reverse, back
into the past, 1880, looks like we've arrived
at the Belle Epoque – a much shorter lifespan, no
hot showers, syphilis a problem (wait, don't
describe the cure), but, look, there's Lautrec
& there's Degas &...
                        for starters: gun-shy & then
we'll move ever onward to Appalachian
supernumeraries & that *fait accompli* guy
who gags at speed, a Fast Eddy teaser
that will keep Claude guessing for twenty-
seven years.
                Is it fear of the nineteenth wheel
or just of those Colt .45s for sale in the five & dime
that prompt the man with the mother spiel to gift us
with his take on Singing Sammy Ward? We'll
never know & I for one don't really care. If
I'm going to get upset about anything it will be about
those ribbons on Uncle John's chest &, as stated
above, the gunk on the sheets & the short life span...

Ward Seven
Who's for ward pride?
If not by the light of a maid's lurks
we're paged by what? Number mad with sane
& the Molly you think so fair is a face
for an apricot fan. All
of her curtsies at once, at once, all
of her curtsies at once.
                In a cup
I thought empty the blood of an owl, for who

has wit enough to keep at bay the hounds
of Henry the Eighth, his double
I'm forced to shave. Bury me not in the lap
of a dog, I said, & he did not listen, in the lap
of a dog & he did not listen.

                    In father's piano
with the lid nailed shut, that's where I'll be when Henry's
finished with me while his cooks skim off
a right keen breast (a ripe queen's breast), & so
they should for it seems that glaucoma thugs
are close behind, are close behind
with rags for eyes.

                 At most
in trams I trust, a dozen dozing
in a depot, in each the corpse
of a man like me who all too soon was quick
through hospital corridors tangled like baobab roots
on the verge of marrow, on the verge of marrow
those baobab roots.

                  If by tooth not nail
I judge a hunt those dogs in the thick
of shamed men will be kicked by him
who's for ward pride; for it was him I'm sure
who left a knife on my kitchen table, to do
what with, a knife on my table
to do what with?

                Not the wit
to know, not wise like an owl
that left its blood in a cup for a queen
to find, to make of it a broth
to quiet Henry's hounds at large
in tangled roots, in tangled roots
at large.

             And for a finale
we turn to the last page (sane
numbered by mad) where a surly nurse
with ten thumbs is dressing my eyes
with ribbon, an obstreperous rainbow
skipping its maid on the verge of marrow, its maid
on the verge of marrow.

128

Oz Hardwick
United Kingdom

... to Station

So, when the doors close, that's it: the end of everything, whether there's a new beginning or not. I've never made plans, and it's too late to start now, so I begin by listing my assets: credit card, debit card, £48.67 in cash, along with a few euros from a recent holiday, the clothes I'm sitting down in, all of my own teeth, a remnant of my hair, a few extra pounds I've never managed to shift and have just got used to, and a tall – maybe 2ft, or perhaps a touch more – domed cage in which is perched a canary. The train's pretty crowded, so I have to hold the cage on my lap, which means looking at the woman opposite through twinned bars. It's like she's visiting me in prison, and I wonder if she has a file in a cake, or perhaps a confession of an affair that nobody wanted to happen, but it did, and she tried to wait for me, but she couldn't, and it breaks my heart but I can't blame her, and I can't hold back my sobbing any more, and she leans forward ... She looks at the canary, and then at me, and I see that she's crying, too, and so is everyone in the carriage, and the ticket collector is weeping and handing out tissues with neat holes clipped in each corner, and the canary is singing like I've never heard before.

Protocols for the Nuclear Family

We hide the children beneath the floorboards, with the mouse-crimped picture books and fashionably dropped consonants. It's an Aladdin's cave down there, or Frankenstein's laboratory, or a bank vault primed with laser trip switches, or a catacomb of cancelled androids. Tea lights barely tickle the dark, and an alley could be an eye down there, observing the infrared, and the furniture's surely fingers, stacked to the ceiling and clicking. The children don't ask why, having known nothing else since they were sperm, egg and desire; but they're curious about who we are, with our doors and windows, with our complex relationship to light. It's a question I sometimes ask myself and, although we never speak of it, I know you do, too. And who are these children? Were they here when we moved in? Were they here before the house was even built, when the street was nothing but wheat and the shadow of a five-sailed windmill? What do they do in the darkness? Do they remember?

Shedding

Snakes come by to shed their skin, drawn to the warmth of my hearth and home, with its embers of remembered conversations and glowing souvenirs jostling on the shelves my dad put up in the 70s. Some of them are poisonous and some could swallow a curious schoolboy whole, but we came to an agreement early on that we'd leave each other alone. Sometimes we'll meet in the kitchen, or waiting on the landing outside the bathroom, and they'll ask me about my writing and I'll ask them what snakes think about all day. I confess that I'm writing about them, and they tell me they dream about me. It's a kind of love that's touched by fear and – we fall silent as we consider archetypes and the conjunction of all narratives seen through a telescope as they eclipse a collapsing star – the only possible response is art. Snakes write songs we'll never understand, that will never make the charts and will never be edited to sell perfumes or boot-cut jeans, yet we'll hum the tunes as we tinker with cars or wait for distant relatives to pick up the phone. What they do with my words is their own business, but when they leave, I stuff pillows with their crisp skin so I can listen to the hiss and whisper of scales stroking scales.

Bee

Bee is king of plants and armies, woven from the multiple strands of crops that, with many offspring, are the handsomer scientists of the world. Bee has subtle wings and great skill, gathering honey with which he wages war. Fleeing from smoke, Bee declares that corpses of plants need the kingdom of love. As one of wings, Bee matters because, whatever the food we eat, flesh establishes new habitats for wild numbers, and today the industry is in bloom. However, Bee subtly contemplates the forms of various flowers, weaving wax into serious penitents with small eyes. Bee's colour is bright, but natural historians tell us there are 250 gods: and for the pesticides that have better workers, this heavenly earth could be a contributing factor. As it is, Bee finds scientists' houses empty and idle, black and in major decline. This is important because the Devil should not infiltrate flowers, pollinating a third of pests and diseases which have been linked to causes of severe memory loss in fixed populations. Bee is transformation. Those who, irritated by noise, do nothing for the moment, are an increasingly grave danger because of the decay of the putrid. Bee is in the world.

Time and Tide

Dragging the rope as tight as you could, you showed me what

you'd hauled ashore: a few fish and the expected plastics; dull corals and a World War I aeroplane. I was never one for marine biology or combat aircraft, so I asked probing questions about carrier bags and milk bottles: is there an international consensus on check-out remittance, and do mermaids recognise the significance of red, blue, or green caps? Our conversation limped along, you weighing up your answers, limbs taut as hawsers and brow furrowed with contemplation – or maybe just the strain of millions of tons – as I pretended to care; and all the time the aeroplane's pilot stared barnacle-eyed at the sun he hadn't seen for a hundred years or more. *I have seen sand fuse to glass*, he said, his reef-jagged voice clipped and formal, *and turn again to sand. I have held the weight of others' dreams and sorrows. I am no Icarus, but nor am I the Angel of Death.* Your hands were smoother than I expected, white as milk or swans' feathers, unfamiliar with war shopping.

Nicholas Alexander Hayes
United States

Apologia
Lush lavender labia
spill into the canopy
softening the sun.

Epicurus tucked into
the fur lined chamber
of an orchid

asks for a second
draught of vintage

before fading from answers
and agony.

His body left to hollow wasps draped
in violet velveteen
striving to be real.

Keeper
Huddled against moss, the keeper of the forest dampness
pulls his feet from river bank mud.

Time ticks out in currents.

Small white flowers scatter from the canopy.

This goblin king weaves
nests for therianthropic
song birds while waiting
for glitter
to biodegrade.

The keeper of the forest dampness-
not brave but honest- is
a tumult of static around the pure chords of love,
seeking the way but not the path,

wind that brings storms but never rain,

fire that never catches.

Dominique Hecq
Australia

Unfinished Genesis
>   *To follow knowledge, like a sinking star*

Wave-sounder and I dropped out
of the sky the day the earth stopped

breathing. Now we live underground:
inside a volcano dotted

with mushrooms, some as large
as saucers, others little larger

than pinheads. Mosses, lichens
liverworts line our lab. We work

like clockwork to the rhythm
of the universe, looking

for non-verbal signs swimming
in our galaxy—a message

from before the Big Bang. Some would
say we're fishermen in the sea

of stars, or poets of the cosmos
zooming in on millions

of light years and new ways
of making sense of waves.

Outside the volcano is a space
port, just in case we hear a chirp

from the Archaean, or beyond
the origin of god's breathing

Bob Heman
United States

She
Guns are not the nascent splendor of the republic. He quotes the futurist
colonel whose ashen limbo respects opium and innuendoes. He is futile
and prepaid, ineligible for the pamphlets or washtub. She has come to
inspect his forestry. She is not moaning, infirm, or going. Her shadows
budget nativity only to those proving loyalty. He flogs the cutlery and
marshals the phrenetic schoolboys to repay the sardines. She is incognito,
napping amidst the lozenges, siphoning loopholes from his herbal
opulence. Symbols abound in their marshy guidebook. He reflects
syllables and swims pallidly through the inky entrails. They are cordial,
mispronouncing philters and lotions. The vendetta supplements their

133

repossession, restricting only their postures. It is noise in the hemlock. She meets him halfway.

Noon
The spittoon was peerless, splashing the immense sobbing volcano with platonic greetings. Its feeble lantern launched the mutant up the gushing ladder, lending compassion to the jostling protozoan that was profaning the opium navy. Precaution moaned in its waspish lotus, honing the saucy membrane to a radiant minaret. A parakeet was muttering gauze flowers to all the spastic nuggets. It was hungry for oxides and love.

Hat
The hat keeps latent midgets from operating on your paranoia. Monkeys watch from a safe distance, hoping to avenge their chastisement. The opposite of the mud is always the minister. Their game founders in the epistemological jungle that implicates our furious beginnings. The hat mutates into something gigantic that occupies the entire sky. From its angle something frightening is born.

William Heyen
United States

The Tooth
After the beheading, they found
the one gold tooth in Custer's mouth.
They propped open his jaws,

cut away his upper lip,
& stared into the tooth in firelight.
It was like a small television

tuned to the news, & a white man
in a white suit was already
stepping down onto the moon.

California Ear Prophecy
Custer's right ear was plugged,
stopped up with cess, as he put it.

134

He tried snapping his neck, tried
stomping on his right foot, but
nothing dislodged the dam until

one night he slept on it & heat melted
congealed wax & everything poured out:
pubic hairs, a ruby Libbie had lost,
treaties on parchment, patches of red skin,
cherry trees, cannonballs, Coke cans....

It got so claustro in his storage facility
he had to move, & Libbie with him.
They accelerated toward a rainbow scum
beyond the Rockies, taking everything along: TV,
McDonald's golden arches, & Yankee Stadium.

Jack Hirschman
United States

The Surrealist Arcane
In Memory of Anais Nin
1.
It's over, Anais, you know,
    the surrealist affair.
Its *Last Will* and *Testament*
    shows Artaud went mad,
    Breton grew old,
a little flurry in the air
    now and then,
    here and there:
a few underground pamphlets,
    an exhibition,
    a journal peppering
America with shouts about
    what we know is true,
THAT WE NEED PURITY LIKE
    NEVER BEFORE!
    But for all intents,

and violence,
it's over, Anais,
you know.

That's why I hold you dear.
You're why surrealism
must have been a woman
with an ageless dream
that keeps on stripping you,
keeping you
young and refreshing
to hear and read.
Which is why, after three
times together, three
times I've wanted
to write a Manifesto
in the key of D,
resurrect the Tarot as the only
means of knowing,
launch an unintelligible
movement with the green
ink taken from
your eyes.

2.
Listen, you must
listen, you
must listen to
what I have to say.
Give me even just
one of your lapels.
You must
listen!

Here, where I find
myself now,
where I'm clear
as a bell,
I wasn't before.
What I have to tell,

please, I beg you,
　　　　listen!
3.
Author!
Encore!
Author!
In your reality I'm dead.
In your reality I went mad.
Suiiiiii
ciiii
ded.
In your reality buffooned.
By your reality condemned.
To
Ro
Da
Fo
Nine
Years
La
Bor
Now I'm opera and book,
now I'm knife at your back.
The acts of my hell are over,
the act of my life begins.
Before you: the spectacle of me.
On all sides the spectacle of me.
My ensembles will initiate you,
show you the perennial flower
at the heart of your insanity.
It's the end of cliche seasons
with fragrance of a new holiday.
In one act I'll break into your skin
and bring your house of organs
down, down, and let the infinite
loose in your blood and make
the ritual chaos of anarchy sing.

Heikki Huotari
United States

Scenic Overlook 2

Though I'm unable to absorb it by osmosis, moss is positively plausibly maroon. In flashy camouflage they brandish tiki torches. Alternate realities obtain.

No matter that it's on the moon, my footprint is protected by an act of congress. So be spiritual My Adviser, be both first and last to call. As on the eve of alteration, to an ear the sea not sleeping, motors turning over and the better angel of the intersection granting rights of way, should jokes be told or told and old the secret service will investigate.

The interval with endpoints (a,b) and (c,d) consists of all points (x,y) such that x is between a and c and y is between b and d. My hiding place and personal experience are yours.

Scenic Overlook 4

Santa Claus and anti Santa Claus are in agreement: after mastering simultaneity, time travel is a snap. Reality is what most matters. Colorado long ago forgave Balloon Boy's parents.

Walking upstream, counter to the earth's rotation, every comment thread devolves to Hitler with some would-be influencer's big brain on display. Year Zero is that of the death of god and neither compasses nor crumbs will show the way.

Time travel is a snap. As isotopes past half-life we are asymptotically approaching one of many linear accelerators. Mortals none the wiser, with a pattern and an anthem I hereby deduce the seventh day.

Cindy Huyser
United States

Recipe for an Invisible Cake
Dark matter admits
no longing gaze as the black hole
steers gas from its accretion disk, steals
from its stellar companion. Silent
spheres swerve the orbit of each

spider's eye, the octave of them.
Lightlessness spells its name mass.

Articulate arm with six degrees
of freedom measures every element.
The kiln we call summer, baking.
The walk-in we call winter, icing.
Beyond that dim limit, the event
horizon, an invisible cake
can't be rising.

Helen Ivory
United Kingdom

First Born
After a picnic in the park
my mother gave birth to an egg.
At the hospital they placed it in an incubator,
and the midwives held vigil.

Her mother said
it was the tuna paste being 'off'
and didn't believe the fanciful story
involving the swan and the roundabout.

On the day of the hatching,
the sun rose as usual and my grandmother
took her customary bus to the hospital
with grapes and Lucozade.

The next day my mother took her bundle home,
oblivious to the entourage of swans
massing in the sky above the bus.
The baby looked like any other newborn.

My Mother's Room
She is uncertain if the room
is the hidden architecture of sleep

or if its walls are made of real plaster and straw.

So she walks the house every night,
along corridors that vanish like thieves
soon after the sun appears.

There is a singing that shines
from a closed door
but she can't move the handle.

There is a kind of singing that turns winter on its hinge
that wakes animals from their long sleep
and places birds on the highest shelf of the sky.

My mother listens intently,
but with her ears turned to caves,
it's all echoes.

The Family at Night
We were ragdolls after school
and passed long winter evenings like this:
father in his armchair with an unlit pipe,
mother in the kitchen pretending to eat,
my sister and I with our small occupations.

We saw little with our button eyes
and spoke even less with our stitched-up mouths.
We played at playing till it was time for bed
when mother sewed our eyelids down
so we could get a good night's rest.

We always woke as our human selves
to find the downstairs rooms had altered too.
A chair unstuffed, a table's legs all wrong,
and, that one time, kittens gone from their basket;
the mother's bone-hollow meow.

My Two Fathers
When my father removes his skin

he steps to one side and tidies
the old skin away with a dustpan and brush.

He wants nothing more
than not to make a spectacle
but my mother insists he fill it with stones.

The stone father is anchored
to the armchair, while the other
goes upstairs to his room in a sulk.

The stone father holds the television control,
orchestrates the night's entertainment.
The other stays asleep like a bear.

The House of Thorns
after Alice Maher

It takes no more than a word
for a flame to stir in its womb
for smoke to rise and push at the walls
like a trapped and injured beast.

There is no chimney, no window,
no gasps of air, so the fire that's grown
too big for the hearth
will die before it eats up the room.

Here is a bed for the wolf,
here is a chair burst at the seams
and here's the little pot
that will cook and cook and cook.

*

It's hard to imagine a path from this house
when you can't imagine a door.
The roof is braced against all four winds,
you're swaddled inside a coat of thorns.

There are stories about spring mornings,
about dew-soaked grass,
the signature of your footsteps;
you, the only child on earth.

The house is blind to romance;
makes you pin down your tongue;
rocks you till you fall asleep
hush-a-bye, hush-a-bye, hush-a-bye.
*

When the seeds are planted
and the roses are grown
mature enough for a harvest of thorns
and all the effort of building a home
tattoos neat scratches
on your parents' hands,
now, think of a house.

Think of another house
a house of your own,
cut from the cloth of your very own skin.
The thought rises up
like a singing clock;
its bird constructed
of feathers and springs.

Gerald Jatzek
Austria

camera obscured
this is the movie you wanted to be
part of
          cast: iron
cutter: the man with the axe next door

this is the way you wanted the hero:
barbed

          wire around his neck
a dolly
          grip
          on a welfare cheque

this is the story you wanted to trade
in for good
          friday nights
bright city bright fights

Michael Jennings
United States

Today Perhaps the Lizard
who lies down in his own shadow,
inventing the sun through half-closed eyes,
feels his skin, thickening with years,
grow nervous as water.
Perhaps he just feels lucky.

You keep coming back like a dream.
Your hips make light shiver,
make me peer up silly-sideways
like an old dog
to watch the bonfire of your bones.

Night's coming, though.
The sky-blue water
of your eyes will turn dark
 then. Stars will come out.

Tomorrow
you will come and go again
like a river—
your bright bones
                    stealing my shadow.

Where She Dances
Purple jaguar midnight
of lost imaginings—ebony, jet,
obsidian lakes of fire—
hers are the drumbeat spanking of bare
hard feet, far off wafting of laughter.

Come dance with the daughter
of rag-tag summer. See the turn
of her fiery wrist. Moon
paints her shadow. Sun
cannot find her. The fierce stars

bring her to bliss.
Once she was tree trembling in moonlight.
Once she was river
tied down by her hair.
Once she was wind, once she was breath—

now only flame
in the flare
of a pupil,
a delicate rustle's
velvety purr.

When the River Flutters
her wings, she is no longer the Amazon
floating the crescent moon as her navel,

she is your shadow rising to meet you.
The nightsilk mountains bend close.

Something in the lisping silence grieves,
exalts, dies its thousand deaths.

Your body is also a river with wings,
with talons, a place of betrayals

where shadowy gods, horned

or with twisting serpents for hair

are drowned, torn to shreds,
then rise again into stars.

Tomorrow, at dawn,
something shaggy will come down,

peering out from the night-drugged leaves,
dazzled by the spokes of new sun.

Andrew Joron
United States

The Person
But, I have only ever seen The Person–my counterpart–against the grammatical background of interstellar night.

He stands at my door, little realizing the *zero* of predicate is one, while the *prey* of predicate is two. He will say only the errata: *red*, at war with itself; *blue,* always the last instance of blue.

The Person wears a headdress, a dress of thought.

The Person is male with female characteristics, fallen into autumns of stain & substance. His sin is a cinema of seeming, a body-sign of *both* & *neither* meeting, teeming.

The Person wears what is: a "melancholy cloud." My closed system.

His signs point backward. His eye wants what it cannot have.

Taste waste, the One without mouth, the Eye ever over I.

Icon of the blackness of Blankness, icon of the whiteness of Witness.

Cite I, seer: O deafened hour, defend ear.

145

My, my, cold, cold, pyre a poor evaluator, & "alive" a lottery of lit particulars.

Because the sun dies in eyes, day is all Idea: a phosphorescent nightscape of skin & bone.

The start of art is always too soon or too late. My statement corrected, as sonically connected, gives only what cannot *not* be given: the empty set, once pieced together; the ware of whereness once aware.

Depart, part: pay per sun; pay per perishing, shadow—

The Removes
After the Time Epidemic, the eyes of owls were found embedded throughout the soft balustrades, reminders of —

A fateful plan your cellmates (in this centuries-wide prison, whose actual walls have yet to be discovered) will soon deploy against you —

This is understandable. You are waiting to achieve your paradigm, a damaged star. Running like smoke from the Chamber of Ills, your signature commences —

"Against the operations of chance," you write, "it is sufficient to call upon the sign of the Umbrella, that which opens outward, or the Sewing Machine, that which stitches together — inasmuch as meaning will be defined systematically as a series of openings and closings upon the dissecting table of Language."

Thus, the words of your confession appear as vestiges of an Original speechlessness, ragged holes in the firmament —

"What phoneme in *integers* is also present in *jewels*?" — Why answer? The laws of thermodynamics can't forgive you because your name is a darkened festival of sound.

Here, then, is the gift of your exhaustion — a precious animal stroked to transparency.

Here, too, is a windowless sunset — its proof scratched out by the charred branches of your eyes.

Your pursuers, inevitable, still trust in the parallelism of acts where desires converge. Yet space itself must be spoken aloud, the emanation of a veil. . .

To the Third Power
The cube is very stable upon the table.

The cube is the remnant of a perfect thought.

The vertices of the cube both control and conceal its power source.

The faces of the cube contain an innumerable swarm of points, ready to rebel against the eight privileged points that stand at its vertices.

The map of the cube shows an ocean at its center.

The cube is a continuation of chaos by other means.

Each face of the cube sees only its opposite as its mirror-self; as if ashamed, the other faces slant away in perspective.

The faces of the cube, the phases of the moon.

The cube is a box of eyes.

The cube is a six-legged insect trapped in abstraction.

The cube is the trumpet of an angular angel.

The point at the center of the cube incubates triangles.

The cube, as a closed system, is always cooler than its surroundings.

The cube is a garment dropped at the door of eternity.

The sex of the cube is the number six.

The cube, so rigid in all its relations, reeks of eros.

The brace of the cube is the embrace of pyramids.

The cube is a citadel standing at the end of history.

The cube wants only to rest here.

Nature does not want to make a cube.

The cube is a necessary accident; the cube is the wreckage of risk.

The cube is displayed before royalty as the last of its kind.

The cube is commanded into being, as formlessness laughs.

The cube, in order to be understood, must be floated in midair.

An old man walks into a cubical white room and notices his footprints reproduced on the ceiling above. He finds he cannot exit the room. As he paces, the pattern of his steps continues to be traced on the ceiling until it has been completely blackened. He stops and looks up into the pathless black.

(Hint: there is a mathematical solution to his plight.)

The Phrases of the Moon
Full

     the blow to a gong
—gone blind

     with the sight of white
Silk, O milk
     of my reason—

     sun reseen in
My mad mad mirror.

Gibbous

Sense
Less science: the

Wish-apparition of a perfect fact.

     As thought, the war
Of one upon one.

Half

Half a mind almost mine.

Whole
     fragment, I am
A being from another word.

Crescent

Bow bent back—to what release?

     My lone line, the join of all I am not.

A minor truth betrays
A major one—
A lore
          for the lyre.
For it is written: *liar* with a *why*.

New

          Calling all coincidence, I will
Deem the dark my day.
Yet—if I say
          I am lying, I am lying
To you now.

O zero raised to zero—I am lying with you now.

Tim Kahl
United States

How True Love Prevails on Bombay Beach
A balding man booms commands into a bonfire and a love
          story
is thrust upon the Swiss. The boy and girl are shy about
          kissing

since April came tangible as the shade and the sand in ancient
          masonry.
Old Northern winters have warped the earth beneath and urged
          volcanoes

to erupt. Dark plumes intrude upon Bombay Beach and a
          million birds
listen to the sediments crunch—part of the planet's ballet of
          grey dust.

Over there the popular gods are considering their movie
          budget
and questioning the sexual orientation of the sky.

The perfect outdoor backdrop shows a brick house covered
      with mud
made in the garden by a dozen herders honoring the horse-
      demon weed.

Slowly a song pulls the owls toward peace—like Hindus and
      Muslims
sticking the landing and throwing a bouquet of white flowers

to vanish beneath the sea. The rising swells cancel the
      wingbeats,
cancel the scavengers, cancel the water politics of the
      blooming deserts,

cancel the dunes in the moonlit distance where life hinges on
      small decisions.

This is the reason jazz has died because of all these little
      repetitive

motions and gestures. The middle manager of makeshift minds
has finally decided on a plot . . . what does a camel do in

the middle of Delaware City? No one lives in the ZIP code
      there
except for credit card companies and the ceremonial blood
      donors.

Wolf Lichen Nocturne
The river water flavor from the rough country bests the bitters
      in the yolk.
Ancestors of the reeds and toads step through shadows to
      reach the oral mulch.

Sun spurs are thrown off into the museum video and urge fire
      in the snout.
The dragonfly shrine on the California State Seal replaces the
      stallion glyphs.

Raven song is reported by the data children on
        the ocean at Fort Bragg.
A lonely thread of sage scrub tests negative for sprawl on the
        coastal cliffs.

Acorns in the Cracker Jack, a pellet in the psyche of the oak
        and gray rat
that traces the dents and black discs in remembrance of the
        inoculated trees.

The Holocene dunes align and shift their awareness to the
        exotic tides of ice plant.
Valley ladybugs and redwood burls escape from the mafia
        grass that persists

as if a wild blue god climbing the ladder in the rapids to soil
        the old willows
whose canopy sags, whose granite is gathered in the sweet
        scent of sycamore root,

redirected into shallow bedrock by the trends in the terrace of
        clouds.
In contrast, the pure quartz sand reappears in the quail's high
        canyon voice

in the silhouette of the pointing dog and the thrashing salmon
        earnest as all Ohlone.
Imagine them now interrogating the claypan and the tussocks
        turning in the dust,

part of tarweed and brown conifer returning to float along the
        egrets
in Holy Slough where the weather's extreme bias conspires
        with a volcano.

So much for the old habit of shrink and swell, the cracks are
        deepening
and the wolf lichen extends its nocturne and sharpens its beaks
        and horns.

George Kalamaras

United States

Nikos Engonopoulos Listens to Jacques Prévert's "Autumn Leaves" and Weeps

Quicksand slid into the back of his throat
There was an ocean in that mud, he knew,
But also piles of dead hummingbirds
He didn't know how to speak them
Back into life
He contemplated their wings
Begging some pauses in the song to sink them
From his throat down into the sea caves
Of his chest
Where he might repair the feathers and heal
Their flight
Everywhere he turned it was autumn
The spring lilacs
Summer lightning
Christmas snow blistering the plane trees
Then came his mother's cancer
The way he rubbed her feet that week to ease her unrest
And his own
Then came his older brother, Athanasios
Dead from diphtheria
His father's gauzy eye
The time in bed with his first wife in the moon's half-light
When she told him she was pleased, but he did not believe her
He remembered Jacques Prévert
And their days in Paris
Cigarettes together at the café
Joking with Desnos, now dead
With René Daumal, gone
And René Crevel, also gone, though by his own hand
And Antonin Artaud's bit lower lip
Tristan Tzara's monocle
And days painting together with Giorgio de Chirico
Piles of dead piles of birds
Which he knew to be hummingbirds

153

Because of what he missed in the middle of the song
The throbbing wings the song evoked
In ways in which they were melancholic but gone
Gone the days of Athens cafés and art exhibits
Gone the dreams of writing of painting his dreams
Into a world he believed
Could be changed
When words in a sentence merged
When vexed verbs and the right noun
Cunning curves and color
But there persisted Prévert's "Autumn Leaves"
On the phonograph
Round and round like the seasons
Those leaves
As if they were barely holding barely clinging
To their russet their gold
Trembling
Falling
Sinking
With the birds
The piles
Of dead piles piling
Into the ground that he knew
Both bore him and would someday soon consume

Apparently Hector Kaknavatos
with a first line by Kaknavatos

Apparently it could not be otherwise
Apparently the kerosene lamps had been set in your chest
Apparently even your mathematics could not save you
And the onslaught of the junta tore your tongue
You looked in the mirror and saw a land of blood and hooks
You were Chiron, the superlative centaur, the wounded healer
If the wind in your throat had not been blood
If the blood nets had not been lowered into the sea
If your chest had not been a crowded school of trapped fish
Apparently, though, it was
Apparently it could not be otherwise

154

Apparently when it tried to be, even your chest was only half
Half horse half man the third half an unpunctuated phrase
Leave the commas aside, you pleaded, *Allow the world its mouth*
The last instant recanted, including the pauses most needed
Otherwise, it could apparently not be
Not apparently could it otherwise
Not in Oulipo and its mathematical madness
You turned to Surrealism you turned to myth
You were the son of Titan Cronus and the sea nymph Philyra
How could your body have been half horse?
Your poems, Hector, had *grown* hoarse among the Colonels'
Manly stance
You were smart to hide your mustache
To clean your ears with tobacco leaves, to clone your toes
You stood against the wind crowding your owl
And the forest on fire in the kitchen sink
Apparently it could not be otherwise
Apparently your Surrealism would have lodged in their throats
Declared you decoded of letters not to be trusted
Declared you once and for maybe
You were named for a Trojan prince, greatest warrior of Troy
You were said to have killed 31,000 Greek warriors
You—Hector—could only be killed by Achilles himself
What rose in him, centuries before, from heal to heart?
What caused you to be reborn half horse half man?
To be reborn in 1920 as Hector Kaknavatos, the poet?
You have largely and not, mostly and more
You have mostly not been forgotten even when you have
You have lit the kerosene lamps in the watery chests of fish
Known the sea because a sea nymph gave you suck
You called her *mother* you called her *phrase without a pause*
You knew the enchantment of lamps the burning word
The wick the match we carry inside
In our mouths is housed the beginning of all sound
The ear and vowel lodging of pain in the loud of the mouth
Oh Hector, oh Kaknavatos
Oh Ektor, spelled the ancient way as a tunneling within
You have been waiting for the poem to mouth you into sound
You have been waiting in our land of far too few—and words

155

Below ground the pound of the indignant sea
Below ground your casket and its sway
Apparently it could not be otherwise
Apparently it could not be
Apparently it could and couldn't and maybe still can't
Like all things Surrealist
The fortuitous meeting of Hector, Achilles, and an umbrella
The chance of horse and man on the dissecting table
Like you Hector Kaknavatos
Like your mathematics disguised in the tamp of a lamp
Where your voice wisely hid those years from the Colonels
So that you could be with us now and forever
Hector Kaknavatos's word without end—again

On E. Ch. Gonatas and the Origin of the Mirrors of Our Being

She had hanged tiny mirrors on trees for the birds to
look at themselves.--Epameinondas Ch. Gonatas

Here we go again, trying to see ourselves.

Let's say there is a forest raised on wolves' blood.

Let's pretend the lightning loves us. That we will burn forever.

Let's promise our mouths that we will one day speak without speaking.
That our insides will remain inside.

That Lautréamont's sewing machine and umbrella never met on the
dissecting table but in the copper gutters of our throats.

E. Ch. Gonatas knew this. Knew enough to avoid dust from the sirocco
coming in across the sea. Knew that it did not originate from tropical air
masses, as he'd been told, but from abrasion inside animal dung fueling
fires in the Sahara.

Yes, in the early days, he often met with Embirikos. With Hatzilazarou.
With Engonopoulos. Elytis. Gatsos. Sachtouris. Kaknavatos.

Of course, he founded *Primal Matter* with Papaditsas in '58. Splitting open a pomegranate sizzling throughout our blood.

Who in their right mind requires more than one name? Gonatas thought.

Even each of the Nine Muses stood solitary. Bemused.

There is one speck of fire. One confused botfly in the horse's nostril.

Life could be beautiful, he thought, *as the fortuitous meeting of a botfly and hemostat in the silky underarm hair of the Belovéd.*

Lautréamont, Gonatas knew, would be pleased.

Might beg the birds to peer into the tiny mirrors they took as one another's mouths.

There is no point in saying it right.

We must persist in saying it right.

How could Gonatas have largely been forgotten? His poems stranded in a ditch in a mixture of broken branches, possum blood and road salt?

The origins of how it all ends lie in *The Book of Perfect Eternity*.

Seeketh the advice on pages 109–113 in a one hundred-eight-page book.

Sometimes even letters and numbers mix, in a confusion of mouths. Stunted mirrors buried inside the bodies of birds.

That with which we speak flies into the kerosene lamps and singes letters of the word *mouths* off into *moths*.

Brother-my-sister. Say *no* when you mean *yes*.

Say *E. Ch. Gonatas* when you mean *Epameinondas Ch.Gonatas*.

Blur the names of the Muses as you might bend the night bones breaking during the turbulent winds of sleep.

I say *Thalia*, Muse of pantomime and pastoral pain, when I mean *Clio*, Muse of history and dead horse bones.

I say *Calliope*, Muse of epic agonies, when I mean *Urania*, Muse of astronomy and the belly-burn of stars.

I say *Polyhymnia* when I am speechless in a forest of wolves' blood. Amidst wind-ripping. In a moment of startled lightning. When at last I reach the Sacred Word inside my *own* saliva.

How could one so primal be tossed to the trees?

Oh, Gonatas. E. Ch. Gonatas. Belovéd Epameinondas Ch. Gonatas. You are here and not here. There and somewhere swirling in the mouths of the other four Muses—Erato, Euterpe, Melpomene, Terpsichore.

Yes, "The Autopsy." Elytis closed my favorite poem of his with, *We shall have early fruit this year*.

And I repeat it. Plant it here, again. In you, Gonatas. In the mirrors of your mouth. In termite eggs you laid for us in mounds faraway, which are very close. In the bones of our head as we lie sleeping, awake. Revoking our wrong. Thinking our dream of you and the marvelous moist of your words was only as slippery as smoke and could only last so long.

Inscribed Into Him, Into His *Him of Her*
after Gregory Pardlo

I was born in possum saliva in a hound dog's thumping
of her tail. I was born in swamp water, cypress beards, and cigar
smoke. I was born in a pot of boiling tea, in the words *Gyokuro*
and *Oolong* where I placed the placement of particulars
of why I was named and how. Woke I woke with bobcat bones
broke and slackened back into the porous sore of more and
      maybe
and most. Mostly born, I came unto the world this time
to make things right, to settle the letters of my name, proffer

my expertise of blurring the belly-burns of the stars. I swore
an unexpected vow, then another, then one, three, maybe four
       more,
saying things backwards like ticks grumbling the flesh.
I was born with mosquito madness. It wasn't a disease but gifts
whingeing through me, through *it*, when the pronouns mix. Say I
       was you
when I was me saying something found and lettered and named.
Tea was brought, tea was drank, sprinkled on this root
and that when I was before I was born.
What is *your face before your parents* were *born*,
the monk quieted into me, slipping through me
the swampy dark and saliva spill of the gently cruel animal
night. Hound dogs bayed, the moon crawling from kerosene
lamps. Tea leaves told me time tears me apart, burns me
inside out, life to life, when I am born in the pelvic bones
of a sassafras hollow. When the tea leaves rot, dried
in the shape of a man eating a poisonous pufferfish,
and suggest a world. I was born to be
born each time to test the flesh, Buddhist, Agnostic, a Tantric
fleck mixed with rain in the still ponds
of the *Tao Te Ching*. Born, as I've been,
screaming and weeping to leave the woman's dark
and emerge in sterilized, hospital light, born, broken
yet whole, each time, time and again.

Kingdom of Throat-Stuck Luck
We were at the mercy of not having had anyone in the family
       die.
We sang our song, we committed our talk, and working late
       seemed in our best interest.

I sought everything crummy, an abomination of a raised arm at
       the back of a schoolroom.
Without making a telegram of historical butter, the best we
       could do was share.

Alexandria had been cut off from Egypt for many centuries by
       salt lakes.

We experienced the torturing impact of a candle unconnected
        to the biography of lightning.

When one of us pointed to the moon, it meant, *sprained right*
        ankle.
When someone hacked a hunk of goldfish onto a hanky, it
        meant, *See the brilliant rain?*

Without history we went on wearing sombreros.
We distanced ourselves from hospital corridors and sarcophagi,
        from whiskey-colored wind, from our esophageal
        amnesia.

Time and again we emerged from the kingdom of throat-stuck
        luck.
All we knew was a pale blue light, the advantage of a back
        window, and an ensorcelling phlegm with which to
        coat the long days of the throat.

Eliot Katz
United States

Liberation Recalled #37
Now that even Gilgamesh drinks Pepsi Light, new
        international songs of desire fill the next century's dusty lungs
Global workers study the tune of holy planet shifts, a
        Sympathy Strike lyric rebounds off a satellite dish
National flags are ripped to shreds, fine psychedelic
        handkerchiefs to catch the new flu
Blake's ninth night arrives, when lions roar from deep
        furnaced caves amazed how it is we have walked
        through fires yet not been consumed
As the war of multiple discourses begins to replace daily
        terror of nuclear pocket swords & plutonium hair
        triggers
Reason passion sensation & instinct embrace, poetry's
        saxophone sounds the cosmopolitan call: universal

citizenship shortly awaits all
Acrobatic voters tumble across ancient bugle boundaries to
        march in world literacy's welcoming parade
The endangered owl opens its eyes wide to guide the
        sundrenched carpenter where best to strike the nail
Insatiable whales bark to let the navigator know near which
        rocks the last ship disappeared
An honest wind warms an honest face, the old window blinds
        cry out to be replaced
A shooting star, the world's most renowned astronomer
        announces the galaxy will never be the same
A trustworthy politician, peace through peace, a concerned
        attentive public, a radio talk show designed to end bigotry
The sociology student who dreams herself president awakens
        in control of her cabinet's affairs
A cyberspace doorbell rings, a roving internet with potential
        companion in its sweet adhesive chords
MTV's Top Forty songs convince the world's most stubborn
        rock to pour its cool liquid forth
Divine genitals perpetually replenished, the Milky Way's
        dynamic power restored, desire below completes the
        symmetry above
Supersonic transport jets gravel-dust the earth's forests,
        demineralized soil says a prayer then drinks up
Ghosts of dead cattle call out for soybean seeds, the fastfood
        ballgame is down to its last out
Awake, awake, the melody of those yearning for love can
        now continue until the next comet falls

Anna Keiko

China

The Prologue to a Group of Twenty Poems Entitled the Profound Words Asleep
Underneath the earth in deep sleep,
in an illusory world of assumptions,
the soul trudges to knock on the door of history.

Time cleanses darkness before the rosy dawn rises.

Fragments of memories are recovered forming pictures,
showing the images of our predecessors thousands of years
        ago.
Not many have ever witnessed
the resurrection of spirits in the ruins.

Violent lightning stimulates sleeping hormones;
and the words sprout from the decayed tree roots.
Eyes from the tree branches sparkle and pay tribute from the
        high place.
Tears from the vault of heaven soothe our dry throats.

People suffer from irregular sleeplessness.
They sleepwalk, go through outer prosperity,
but look for belief on the brink.
Swans seek solitude while the sea calls out.

The wheels of time lose their direction.
Fierce winds disrupt calmness and curl up waves.
Violent streams of rain drown flowers just poking out of the
        soil.
Embankment is no longer on shore;
the ocean is no longer there in the sea.

Pain and drunkenness spread wings of dreams.
Branches and leaves grow strongly out of rotting logs.
Postmodernism brims with spirit.
Symbols for decrees fill the paper.
Saliva and salt are cast onto barren lands.

Utterances throughout the millennia permeate paper and ink.
Asleep, the profound words awake from deep inside the walls.
Eyes from the grave gaze out in fright.
Trembling hands stretch into the afternoon sunlight and the
        library.
Dawn and dusk tell.

What's done is done

What's done is done
The unpredictable occurred, the coronavirus,
A storm that could last long,
Is destroying sprouting branches, flowers
Fear is everywhere
Death is close to anyone
A spring of broken dreams
Dark clouds, sadness, tears
The bell struck the sky
Haughty humans are falling
In the black hole they dug.

Translation by Germain Droogenbroodt

S.K. Kelen
Australia

House of Rats

They're up there all right,
in the roof playing scrabble,
listening to scratchy
old Fats Waller records.
They started out
a gang of desperadoes
escaped from a laboratory,
arrived via a garbage truck
up overhanging tree branches
elbowed their way in & soon
the colony is an empire of rats
who eat the insulation batts
chew wires, through the ceiling
to ransack the kitchen
take bites out of everything
& carry off furniture. I can hear them
scurrying with bits & pieces, hammering & sawing:
they're building houses—a model rat town—with
imitation garages to park stolen toy cars in.

163

After munching down another box of double strength poison
the rats are back at work with a vengeance, thump
around the rafters insulating the house with rat shit.
Or hard at love writhing, squealing like sick starlings
or kicked puppies. The weaker explode
and TV screens fill with rats' blood but there's
more where they came from. Teeming over
mountains, down valleys, jamming highways, falling
off bridges to scurry ashore up storm water drains.
Exterminators arrive dressed as astronauts and poison
the house for ten thousand years. It's time to move out.
But the rats have laid eggs in your pockets, stow
away, follow you from house to house.
The curse enters its exponential phase.
Tentacles unwind from the ceiling, dirty great moths
and leopard slugs take over your happy home.
Soon you are a trellis. That's just what the rats say.
I'm down here listening to radio messages,
oiling automatic weapons, building rockets.
Living in a rat's belly.

Kambah Pool
A bend in the river, water's clouded by green mud
Deep, really deep, good for proper swimming.
These days only children see spirit life
Work and play, see a world invisible to adults
Clear and just, a solar system glows every grain
Of sand and kids crush evil in one hand,
Until growing up evil comes again.
The light dappling the water surface
Reveals some native spirits' power
Derives from fireflies. Gumnut babies
Fuss and fight give a lesson how funny
Is the futility of conflict. Children see
That crazy old spirit Pan left his shadow
Hanging from a tree and reflection
Drinking at the river, the old goat's galloped
Way up mountain, leaps cliff to cliff
Grazes on blackberries growing in the scrub

164

Gazes over his Murrumbidgee domain.
All glands and rankness, his shaggy coat
Putrid with the smell of ewes, wallabies,
Kangaroos, still a monster, he'll take
A bird bath later. Dirty musk fills the air
Like a native allergy, tea trees blossom
As he passes, kangaroos lift their heads
Breathe deep his scent and there are dogs, too.
When the kids see Pan they go gulp
If dads could see him they'd beat him to pulp.
You might not see but the musk stench
Wafts on the breeze. Currawongs squawk
The inside-out salute, warble a tone of pity
For the brute. The immigrant god moves inland—
Raucous the cockatoo never shuts up.

Charles Kell
United States

St. James and the Magician Hermogenes
He stares into a face that is not really a face.
No one after lighting a lamp puts it in a cellar.
When the unclean spirit leaves man, he passes through a waterless place.
He stares into a face that is not really a face.
Forgive his sins: what I never believed, what I wish to replace.
Instead of fish a serpent; instead of air a door.
He stares into a face that is not really a face.
No one after lighting a lamp puts it in a cellar.

Doppelgänger
Seconds click feel the exoskeleton
unhinge want to tell you
so I scrawl half notes on the bitten
edges of napkins I believe your eyes
peering through orange-rimmed glasses
faint curve of upper lip
slight way music rolls from
tongue your made-up song:

lice leap upstream, lice swallow, lice dream
people can never change I know
this is the face molded and pierced
the surface is as private as we get
I agree this skin from Berlin smeared
mentholated sprits gray dust from stones
it was here since the beginning a wall
of white the roll & swallow
of dice people never change

Adele Kenny
United States

Elegy for the Man Who Collected Keys
He's out on a limb with tree bark under
his fingernails—again and against that
once real world—secrets strung from star
to star. It was the threat of sunset and
Professor Plum with a 22-caliber book
in the library. A branch's shadow swings
across the house; the statue he broke has
half a face. On the back porch, bugs kiss
the blue light and crack like knee caps.
Dust burns into breath. Shoehorned in
where he doesn't fit, he has nothing to say.

So Much Life
The girl who killed herself, her dog, and son speaks to me.
She tells me that *this* death is only sleep. I'm not sure
what she means—what other death? I stand above her grave,
not knowing if there is a grave (a place to put her—
perhaps just ash, the newspapers didn't say); but, no,

I see her face. Her lips move before the words:
So much life, she says, *is dead before the body follows.*
She looks at me through stippled eyes and, reaching up,
she trims the moon with pinking shears. Light, unraveled,

falls (a perfect circle) around the dog beside her—
the dog's spirit scratches its jaw. I don't know how she
came to be inside my dream or why she haunts me—
I barely knew her. From my front porch, I see the house in
which she lived—the storm door open. Snow that is ice,
that is glass, covers the lawn; the lawn splinters and cracks.

Kerry Shawn Keys
United States/Lithuania

Purusha Says These Lines Go In And Out Of The Body
Circe and Helen adulterated the exegesis while coasting along the
Adriatic.
Number 16 hosts a herd of anemic pigeons.
Then the boar gored a wolf in Prussia.
The tapestry addict left his needles in Walt Whitman's foot,
          went crabbing on a bayou in the Panhandle, and died of
trichinosis in a cove at Crotch Lake in Canada.
Virgil asked Beatrice to put on black lipstick to give herself
          some definition.
Ponder on this: Jews refuse to eat what's filthy; the Hindus
          what's full of bliss.
I will lay me down on my back on the berm simulating a pig
          and a cow.
Who will cast whom out of whose body.
Papier-mâché has lost all memory of hooves, truffles, and
          teeth.
I went to the market. I stayed home. I am a stone. Riddle me
          and I weep.
Beatrice did not put on black lipstick, and Virgil blushed
          from his indiscretion.
The body is corrupt. A grunt will grunt because it grunts. A
          pariah will be first. The moon will marry a poppy
          seed.
The Earth, as Nimrod knew it, will be pierced with arrows
          and given an otherworldly name.
We will feast on mercury.

What is untouchable is inviolable.
Purusha plays polo piggyback with evangelists in the land of
        light.

Coherence
   for N. E. Enkvist

Which bought a river.
Martha didn't paddle across the Delaware in a gray boat.
We watched a waterbug ride a leaf over the moon's reflection.
Over Warsaw the sky is often grey with pathos.
Communism and Capitalism are white and black.
Black cats mediate between different worlds. White cats are
        green.
On the globe under the equator, conscripts read
   the Southern Hemisphere left to right.
Human rights were discussed in the seminar at the
      Veterinarian school.
Volunteers tortured themselves with gonorrhea in Vietnam
      because they didn't wear raincoats.
The Mekong River irrigates corpses.
I remember the convention in Philadelphia.
It's raining.
Who or what is it?
Why do capillaries whitewash the smallprint on the manifest
      destinies of bottled notions?
If it's political karma then aren't you maya, and who stole the
      covenant from the icebox.
To sell the river and buy a Mercedes for my mother.
She sings the hottest salsa.
Ketchup is too sweet in the Jewish ghetto so we use tomato
      paste for Halloween.
The Nationalists complain about the contamination of the
      culture.
Tombstones are used as steps to the wedding-house.
The veil is nylon and inside-out.
Before and after the mummy with the gold filling.
I shaved my head and pretended I was a Mohican.

If you can walk on hot coals through this understory without
making any noise, then you will disappear in the same
way.
It's not raining.

Tony Kitt
Ireland

Looking Upwards
These stones overhead,
comets juggling omens...
What's the distance between nothing
and no other thing?

We eye the sky thinking of a science
to replace it with. Has anybody flown
to holiness from a language?
To bliss from publicity?

You're right, we should have counted
air balloons inside our heads
well beforehand. Do you know
that all our breezes are sung by vultures?

The sky creates cities and dominions.
Under the setting celestial persimmon, somebody
swaps the whole planetarium of glowworms
for a yarn receptacle.

Down the Grete Stern's Well
Women are flying trees
wandering hands of the world

Crosses dream of becoming ladders
The weight of the moon is
too much for you
let's bleach our

biographical blotches

We giraffe through the continent
and take a trainsnake
to the eyes' coast
we fall into somebody's nostrils
and find our way onto a billboard

A spy in the sky
the self-evidence of cages
Hello this is your inner tiger speaking
without a mouth
How far can you go
if you carry non-being with you?

Cages break
into smaller cages

Polonaise
Snow. A takeaway weather
from the sky library. The farm,
seated under the landscape.
No fly, no dig.
Existence, whitesnaking around
prior beings, animals. A sweetmeat smog.
Shadows wearing footprint robes
wander about with walkie-talkies.

Eventuality. Life angles tabled
to the angel cloth. Boxes and boxes
of mouse-quietness. Errors ambered
into the sunrise.

The mud clock clays the Great Thaw.
The voice lights up,
blooms the rooms. Wintry wounds
exhale lifeless saplings.

Log in to your view-finders, to a radiogummy

of your skull. The motherload of dreams
under the moustache-quilt,
a foretaste of purgatory.

Stone
Touch things turned to stone
silhouettes sitting in a circle
their candle eyes
touch your touch

Silent whirlwinds of essence
droplets of crimson and marine blue
juices of anger, panicking corals
What was mine is now detached

Every name has a body
sapphire thieves wear fire
cathedrals enter their minds
Mark the identity blush

Pity never comes back
Grade these granules of havoc
Tetrahedrons of your ages

walk into your walk
How it all turns to stone

Close Formation
A hunter trails a long-tailed consequence.
It is the sixth nightmare.
Children watch eggplants
grow meanings.

Exuberance exists at the exit.
How would you talk to a mind arrow?
What would you give
for a bullet-proof poem?

Seasonal dying is the profession

one should avoid. I'm doing my beast,
and you are doing yours.
Our genes are our engines.

To survive, we'll have to draculise
our story. For how, ask your napalm,
your landmines.
Nobody would CNN us to safety.

A long-lanced consequence haunts
the hunter. Security by mercuriality.
It is the seventh nightmare.
Meaning plants grow eggs.

Noelle Kocot
United States

The Epic of Gilgamesh
Humbaba
My friends, who can reach heaven?

The monster bellows like a river swollen with flood.
Many are consumed in his fiery breath.

My friends, who can reach heaven?

Let us ask the mountain for a sign.
Let us cut the spirits from the cedars.

My friends, who can reach heaven?

To be remembered a man must undergo
The ravages of the eight winds.

My friends, who can reach heaven?

No matter how tall he is, a mortal can never reach heaven;

No matter how wide he is, a mortal cannot stretch over the earth.
Therefore, may Shamash open before my feet the closed road
*

Enkindu
 We climbed the mountain.
 It was enough.
We chased wild creatures over the grassy plain.
It was enough.
We planted grain.
It was enough.
We drew water from the river.
It was enough.
We dreamed the same dream.
It was enough.
We left our tracks in the forest.
It was enough.
You were the shield that protected me.
It was enough.
You were the sword and axe at my side.
It was enough.
You were the ceremonial coat that warmed me.
It was enough.
May the mountains weep for you.
Both night and day.
May the wild creatures of the plain weep for you.
Both night and day.
May the fields overflowing with grain weep for you.
Both night and day.
May the pure Euphrates where we drew water weep for you.
Both night and day.
May our tracks left in the forest weep for you.
Both night and day.
May the dreams that now grieve weep for you.
Both night and day.
You were the shield that protected me.
Both night and day.
You were the sword and axe at my side.
Both night and day.

173

You were the ceremonial coat that warmed me.
Both night and day.

*

Utanpishim

I can see nothing ahead or behind me.
The darkness is so thick, and there is no light.
I go like a murderer, ravaged by the heat and cold.
Why should my heart not be torn apart by grief?

The darkness is so thick and there is no light.
My friend has returned to clay.
Why should my heart not be torn apart by grief?
I do not want to sleep the endless sleep.

My friend has returned to clay.
There are no stars or sun where he is now.
I do not want to sleep the endless sleep.
Neither my sorrow, nor my pleas, nor the tearing of my hair
       could rouse him.

I go like a murderer, ravaged by heat and cold.
I can see nothing ahead or behind me.
Teach me how to build a house that will last forever.
I can see nothing ahead or behind me.

*

Gilgamesh

I am no longer interested in the sword and the bow.
The Faraway has taught me that I am weak.
For whom have my hands labored?
For whom does my blood beat?
My days will soon be washed away like a face drawn in sand.
I have neither friend nor brother by me.
To speak of my despairing mind,
The icy-feathered gulls shriek overhead.
No blithe heart can know what unhappiness I suffer.

Yet I am resigned to all my losses,
And I ask you, my people, to let them touch you.

174

Let me brand my searing path across the shadows before your
      eyes.
Look at the fine temple I have built!
Search the world locked within its stones with a smooth hand!
Throw off the ceremonial coats that warm you,
And shroud yourselves instead
In the raging fire of the answers that never come,
In the raging fire of the answers that never come.
*

Enkindu
What violence has been done to the atmosphere?
See how the stars scurry through the thickets,
Nature's balance broken, and the voices of the creatures
Rise like a spell toward a heaven cast in human fire.
I feel him drawing near; he is anxious to search the world
Buried in me with a smooth hand. I can almost touch his
      features,
The sun-burnt hair curled
Around his toes whispering against my own. And yet what ire
Flames within me when I look upon him in his heart. I who
      have speared
The worst of beasts, who have braved pale seas
As they rose and fell beneath me,
I who have pinned the demons of the night until the haunted
      song of the stricken
Drew its curtains over waves of my pure fury.
Perhaps in this roaring silence, I will embrace the meaning of
      my dream.
*

Gilgamesh
I am tired of the light that dribbles from my voice
So washed in certainty that the days
Will blink like lashes over rich fields of wheat.
I want a place older than the leaves,
Older than these strong walls where the story of the earth is
      carved
Give me a radiance that broods beyond this temple,
Where the hidden mysteries of life and death rejoice
Wildly together, where man, like a dying animal, does not

175

> grieve

After the storms have wrecked his simple
House. I want these things, and yet I will not serve
These idols fashioned out of the same clay
Of which I myself was pinched by my mother's rapacious need.
The very god of storms has wreaked into my first breath the
> secret

That erosion takes patience, not unlike the willingness to bleed.

Compassion IV

The human realities of the living are now
As close to me as my own—oh, see how
Dusty that plant gets when you don't clean
It! The rippling day is a fabulous lesson,
My pants are too loose, and yet. *Bon nuit,*
Mes cheries! All over the whole neighbor-
Hood, your fluid legs move—you are all
Permission and flounce, and your stockings
Catch in the mere light. Perfection, wholeness
Is what I see now in everyone I touch. That
Day when two men came in from the stream,
Wet, bothered, the windows were blackened,
And the cats ran around. Rain came, but
Also sunlight, and the years of hard living
Dissolved. A blanket of verbs crosses the
Threshold. Poetry, you are mine, and I will
Go anywhere with you. A gap in the mind,
A spangled street, my spine, perfectly erect now,
Chooses these words, yet it as if I have no choice.

God's Green Earth

My kinsfolk, I am sorry for my pride.
Are any of us exempt from a bumpy
Road? The memory of each moment,
The greenness of phosphorescent cities,

How they lick the wind. With large round
Eyes I look at the world—look at us all
Dreaming like that! Then, a million

176

Chambers with all of us stuffed in, how

Do we ever foreclose on a menace?
Look at a schoolhouse the color of mud.
See how it tricks itself of its students,
And see what we call a rainbow that

Enwraps all of us in a gigantic circle.
See that blade of grass sprouting up
From a verb, the only one we have
Ever needed, and it is rightly called to love.

Laurie Kolp
United States

Delirium Tremens
As fire sings through trees,
blackberries hang swollen in the woods.

Coiled in a basket of clothes,
dance songs of the bees
embroidered in tight stitches.

Fine music waits in the shadows of hell.
Great bones of my life feel so heavy.

Hollow-eyed, my skin tight to the ribs,
I became formless as fog
just to lounge under the tree.

Keys of the organ assume an immensity.
Let the fire put on its red hat and sing
my eyes, my mouth filling with ashes
newspapers a week old
on a cot by an open window.

Prisms move in the draft my body makes
quick and uncertain

ragged blade of the mouth
somewhere between alcoholism and madness
to the trees whose mouth opens.

Underneath the stairs in a box filled with
violation against the natural course of life
where for a while we went on living [our]
existence a sense of well-being
yoked to the cold, [all]
zing gone.

    An abecedarian cento, sources: Charles Bukowski, Lines 1,6,8,11,
14, 19, 22, 26; Claudia Emerson- Lines 3, 5, 9, 13, 16, 18, 21, 23, 25; Mary Oliver- Lines
2, 4, 7, 10, 12, 15, 17, 20, 24

Michael Leong
United States

from "Disorientations"
[the syntaxes, comet-like, startled
  the earth,
        haloed
        the untranslatable
  foothills
    with vegetable light

      and in the distance—
    the mad, irreducible
        discourse of the surrounding
          mountains

    squatting on the ground,
      I was to find,
          in the indifference of night,
          glimmerings of

  an alien culture
      had appeared
          on our daughter tongue]

We know that the ridiculous "Big-Bang" of philosophy severed difference from difference. But an unsuspected dream trailed interestingly behind in the aftermath: a vision of a head (gazing, ecstatic-like) that can turn the chief concepts of our Occidental fathers into stone. Its Chinese eyes, and other starred features of subversion, suggest and undo us, cause certain Greek letters to appear in the superficial references of our manuscripts.

Constrained by a formal topology, we displace our own subject's upturned person in impossibilities, permitting us to perceive the youngest formulations of modern experience: an enormous new chapter that under no circumstances could be presented in any American or Aristotelian novel. As if to understand the powerful shock of a divine and inconceivable reality in a friend's turnip patch. To discover a whole realm in which everything totters and opens up when sullenly walking. How beneficial to us it would be to descend into the buried articulations of late December, a fictive notion of "nature" muffling the vulgarity of manifest meaning—speech without language, utterance without tongue.

Under active but unknown signs, principal communication was altogether refracted, the dark hair of history pulled up by the root.

*

My teacher said
                nothing is never not entangled
in emptiness.
                Even the perpetual "bullet-like" trajectories
        of the sacred.
                        Or the divided invisibility
of the most visible pyre.
                        The energetic movement
of traffic,
                now forcing   the attending taxis
                                to make a detour,
        is no more
than a system of evaporated streams.

The garlands on the walls
        that ring around the city are falling

                in small
                        illegible clumps.
                                        The eyes
                        under the trees
        have evolved to be less rapid.

            No one thought that the banks would put
                industrial scraps in the mangers,
that the low crest
                was, in effect,
                        an added center
from which the Department of Urban Cancellation
        can irradiate
                        an imaginary *roux*
of *here* and *koko ni*.
                        "Where?"
In the empty well
                behind the pines.
Around
        the abstract roofs
of the Spanish churches,
                whose forms ceaselessly strive
        to order   the vital
                        and aggressive
        calligraphy of heaven.
                Once my teacher rose with a burlap-bag
full of money.
                "Here," he said,
        "let the dharma of modernity
go up in flames."

[NOTE: "Disorientations" collages together—and so "disorients"—two
postmodern Orientalist texts:
Kent Johnson's *Doubled Flowering: From the Notebooks of Araki Yasusada*, a
yellowface simulation of hibakusha (atomic bomb survivor) literature, and Roland
Barthes's *Empire of Signs*, a semiotic treatise based on an invented system
Barthes calls "Japan."]

Susan Lewis
United States

One Day

grass started growing from the young man's chest. *Everybody changes,* said his mother, surreptitiously dabbing at her eyes. But the boy, who was wise beyond his years, felt delicate roots tickling his sternum & knew it was a matter of time before they'd probe his lungs & entwine his heart, crowding the space it needed to expand & contract in its steadfast commitment to preserving his options. As the weeks passed, graceful green strands sprung from his armpits, between his legs, & even, in the finest possible wisps, from his upper lip. One morning he awoke from a luxurious dream of water glossing boulders as smooth & warm as flesh to find a starry sprinkle of tiny yellow blossoms adorning his burgeoning tufts. He had only to be still & tiger swallowtails floated around him, sipping his nectar. Unable to deny the inexorable slowing of his breath, he was content to observe himself contemplate the ramifications of his personal evolution without emitting a watt of excess heat or other sign of agitation.

All Signs

pointed to the same confusion. On the second Monday the third person persevered. Tiny toes like exclamation points, daffodils, or doubts. While the mistress of ceremonies sobbed off the opportunity to introduce her own death. Chanting, mutinous, the girls in our hearts danced on pins & needles, stalking expired goals. Souled like dreaming dogs: backwards sever, forward fever. Naysayers said their. Bed-layers lied. Mixed wintry standards dropped precipitously on the embryonic future poking its head from the earth's gut, while the spicy amongst us inverted our convolutions to the *nth* degree. Out-rhymed, intellect ceded the probabilistic navigation to instinct & its moody henchmen. Lolling yet again on shaky ground, the middle deliquesced to flab & folded.

Tate Lewis-Carroll
United States

I Dreamt Us Having a Pure Son and Father Moment

*A reversed perspective of Kent Johnson's "I Dreamt
Us Having A Pure Father And Son Moment"*

I dreamt us having a pure son and father moment,
too, but near the boundary waters where cross-stitched roots
pull islands into paths. I prepared to listen
by filling swarms of mosquitos
with mantras, hymns, chants, prayers, and blood
sacraments. I counted their bloated bodies
drifting away to spread the news: 7,346,235,014.

When ready, you asked, *What was it like?*
and I opened my ribcage, and you pulled
out enchanted beasts: loons sliding into the muck
to milk their eggs, walleyes floating up the jack pines
to fill their nests with left over fly paper and splintered
ax handles and used handkerchiefs discarded by Eagle
Scouts, ducks with lion teeth, beavers learning
to plant trees in their sleep, coyotes and foxes boxing
on their hind legs, bumble bees with cormorant wings
dancing exclusively against seaweed.
You took them one by one until the magic was gone.

With my cage open I said, *Look in my eyes.*
You looked down, and I knew you knew
how lucidly I saw your face reflected
in the glass lake next to my own. And at that moment,
at once, together, our tears met their rising echoes
in ripples on our cheeks. They rose and rose and fell
and rose.

You tried to convince me these were for me,
always slipping throughout you instead of your rage
then sadness then shame (I assume shame)—
the snarling emptied between us. But tears never curve.

182

We only ever cry into our own reflections.

Clouds below us, the shared space, filled with our penitence.
Then you soaked your palms in my reflection
to cover the distance and dry my face
but you felt foreign, and I felt nothing,
and, this dream, our reaching and drowning
into each other, ever rushing towards its end,
never stopped or changed, either,
no matter how much I wanted to wake.

Bob Lucky
Portugal

The Last Immortal on Earth
In a neat trick theologians still mumble to explain, her parents skedaddled
before she was born. When she called the hospital a few days later asking
for a birth certificate, they put her on hold. She's old now, and although
the seashell no longer roars, she keeps it pressed to her ear like a
telephone. Sometimes she misses the Muzak. When people ask how old
she is, she rolls her eyes and tells them the hospital has her on hold. Her
children think she's crazy, but they love her anyway. She's not going
anywhere.

Afric McGlinchey
Ireland

Night's Three Faces
Cats compose the dark, wrapped
in the weight of night devilment.
They chew on the tale of a fire sister, mutable skies.
There is violence too, in the camber
of voices around the weight of indiscretions.
Cars reverse like a tongue.
A snake cloud. So much to hide.
Every night, the kingdom comes.

The lyric river is calling,
as if the word 'fog' were full of groping shadows.
Rain in the dark, harmonic.
Birds gather oil, sticky and slow.
One flicks up a clot that clips a man cycling
past us, we sit cocooned in a hot car on the pier.
How long can a drowning cat
struggle in a hessian sack?
Or is this just a long night in a room?

Trees bucking, throwing their limbs to the sky,
filling the lungs of a two year old girl
hoisted on to her father's shoulders,
seeing the world from that towering height.
From here, forests can foretell
their own forced breath
cut by the sting of a chainsaw.
I've spent so many hours streaking past
the screaming silence packed below me.

Sonnet in B Major
Sway, everybody.
Even the horse that shies, the child on paper,

green-easy, until flummoxed.
Do magic, like feral creatures turning
quick to a language, cold air awakening.
Coins are still legitimate, but not quiet anymore,
a wet black semi-quaver opening up
the frantic eye of an arbitrary Icarus.
Oh, these bells. But I digress.
If we must die ingloriously, let's first rise up
like snakes from the monumental pit.
We don't get back for a second go.
Speed's got a nerve, a no-time, strident
bunch of followers. All these criminal acts?
Move the iceberg, or lose the Titanic, everything.

A River of Familiars

I have a cat that sharpens her scent on men.
       I netted her from the river, called her mother.

Perhaps there's a cat-flap in the sky;
       sometimes my mother's a golden owl.

I have a memory cat that in a past life
       knew the taste of golden whiskey.

My cat has a curiosity about the whiskey-crazy
       wish for public nudity.

I have a crazy city cat with a lightning dart
       across her lazy eye.

And my lightning cat has an earring – just the one –
       mother-of-pearl. Call it intuition.

And seven secret positions, the last
       a chanting lotus. I have a cat that doesn't exist.

I have a penchant for jumping trains, inhaling
       with each knock. I have a sister cat who inhales too.

I have a lover who becomes a lion under the glassy moon.
       And the cat exhales her wail, like an accordion.

One cat's a grand, glass-lidded, gleaming ivory,
       the light, not yet put out.

First-born, I am, of a cat who cycles lightly,
       inside his mansion full of stories, war and music.

My cat and I wear twenty masks when singing
       out in rain, take it, like a wafer, on the tongue.

I have a cat that sings in white and black,
       or foggy smoke rings, belly up.

As a foggy curtain rises, a missing cat
        runs rings around the time inside a clock.

The Quay of Flames

The small heir blithely bypassed the world,
staked his post to the Republic of Dreams,
screwing together the boards of the first living library.

On the side, two tongues, not an overcoat stranger,
something more fluid: water poured into a vase.
A footing of sinuous little replicas, twisted
into place at 5 o'clock. On the quay,
the limping man drew tiny, counter Xs.
At the turn of the untilled field, his discovery:

a pure tapestry, transposition of estrangement,
resting on adopted terrain.
In rejection, there is luck.

See what happens. Leave the second stone,
turn up curios: the cosmic breath
of a soul taking sideways form.

Preternatural alterities lurk within
furniture, gloomy canopies. They step not twice,
but endlessly, into a wavy river, mingle as one.

Nostalgia is restorative. In any case,
experience the effect.
Plainly see the first day of the world.

Body Notes

Fish swim, oblivious of song
until their body leaves water.
Think of fish sailing
through air, while Lyric
is playing Dvořák.
Think of a pipefish wheel,
watching cumulus journeys:

cloud on the body of sky.

The tall hill is layered with trees,
sun bolting to red.
Think of a rocket, a blaze.
Soldiers on the horizon.
Think of the rack of bodies
as a war machine.
Think of the rhythm of truth
as the rhythm of ricochet.

The room is a suitcase
and does not belong to the doll.
The walls are a swallow of blood.
The stigmata is female.
Think of the notes of her bones.
Think of the pit; think of descent.
This is otherness. Sometimes
the body whimpers.

The tongue is the keeper of flame,
especially when singing.
Think of the tone as a swooning,
nakedness as intuitive.
Think of light through a dream.
Now a body is unlocking a door,
spilling a cup,
blooming with scales.

Bruce McRae
Canada

Biography
I was born at night.
I was born on the floor.
I was born in a snowstorm,
the power cut off,
the woodstove giving up its dead,

a cold wind with its hooks out
and no rescue till morning.

I was born yesterday,
so keeping talking, friend,
keep flapping your gums.
Or better yet, tell me a story.
The one with the wolves in it.
The tale of the headless huntsman.
Tell me how summer comes alive
in the dead certainty of winter.

Giovanni Mangiante
Peru

Tales from a Time After the War
I stand in front of my bisnonno's specter.
His hands shooting forward, and from the top of his skull
a red spider crawls out with scythes for legs.
It crawls to his hands and he draws it to his mouth,
takes a bite, and it cracks like an onion
   "This is all I had to eat before the war."

I cry salted ocean waters as he rips his jacket open
and foghorns protrude from his torso,
shaking the fog-covered room with their roar.
I am seasick. The floor waves in and out
until I drop on my left side. I see him looking at me
   "We threw our dead countrymen under tanks
   so they wouldn't cave under
   the terrain".

I hear the sound of Callao's seaport
bellowing each second a bit closer to where I am.
The red spider drops dead to the floor,
half-eaten, its insides bloody, purplish and white.
Only my bisnonno's hand can be seen through the fog
"Go on",
   He whispers, and I am here.

Aoife Mannix
United Kingdom

Heading Out
Broken piano keys crashing against the coast.
The road whispers west where the selkie
lose their skins and you can taste the salt in the air,
the longing for change electrocuting your tongue.
You are breathing fire as you tattoo the last
of the evening onto a storm cloud.

For so long you were crawling
across broken glass, petrified of the vowels
inside your own name. You kept missing
the steps in a dance everyone else
could speak fluently, but you were out
of tune, screeching, tumbling
into crescendos of confusion.

But now at last you're learning to swim
through these long nights
when the moon opens up the lake
to lost cities. You are arriving
after midnight, bursting with prayers
all the way from Atlantis to let them know
they no longer have to walk on knives.

Not now, not ever. You are the gospel
in the wind, the shipping news
crackling on a radio in a small town
where a boy girl is slicing
their loneliness into thin strips of skin.
The blood pauses because your voice
smells of the ocean.

Lindsey Martin-Bowen
United States

Swimming in Turkey Gravy
To dig objects out of turkey gravy,
listen to the floating silence: there
a rubber duck, whiling away eternity,
backpeddles in water that freezes over.
The frozen lake dissolves into a man
eating mashed potatoes and gravy,
lifting forkfuls from the parquet floor.
Cross-legged on that floor, you sit
and envision strings of white-faced Indians
whirling in Wovoka's dance.
And these clambering ghosts
bring footsteps to your door.
Their knocking teaches you
the overturned pot and the dropped
goblet are gorgeous,
soaking with a duck that gives
the abrupt shriek of glass,
and the house explodes into fire
from burning potatoes and gravy.
Its language of flames
leaves you breathless
in a room where the bed, the chest
and the curtains remain silent,
            inside here,
safe
            from a crazy world.

Agnes Marton
Luxembourg

Sleipnir
Not my hoof! I am swirling,
I am the bandage, I am the scars.

Who else and what for?

190

The don't-you-hurt guys,

the stunt. Coffee with white crime.
Poach as approach, uneasy,

inox traps shining nighttime.

Shaman Boy Kills His Father

I kick your boots from my feet
without connecting nouns to verbs.

Combustible,
just like the greying sky.

I comb it, spell it, call it, swallow it.
Don't count on getting a grandson.

Should they ask where you are,
I will say you have gone hunting.

Anna Maria Mickiewicz
United Kingdom/Poland

Canvas in Cornwall
Heathering city

The evening rotten and yellowish
Sloping

A pear
Falling to the ground
Looking into the depth

The line in the horizon is blurred
In a moment, the red of the west
will shout

Grayness...
The canvas tired with color unveils its nakedness

Regent's Park
He proposed
To invisible clouds
In Regent's Park

And she
Engulfed in sun-trimmed rose muslin
Stepped through doors of glass

One golden step
Under the sky, now draped
Across a steel clock
At the vertices of Victorian towers

One misty evening

Stephen Paul Miller
United States

Tonight
I could become a wafer
and perhaps be transmuted
and the stars could become a leaf
and in the autumn blow away.
Moths could sing in your kitchen
and the world revolve around your lighter,
whole families could cook
dinner in your bread box
so you could get older
and that would interest me too.
The fireplace could be an old museum.
The way you look merits our playing casino
with each match lighting the fire in it.

Evensong
The night air clears my throat.
Even the birds
      sing like Stephen Miller—
      a bird telling a Canterbury tale,
      a bird reciting a love letter,
      a myopic, cussing bird.

I am the loud bird
      singing like Stephen Miller.

These birds are the creation of language.
      but one day
    Stephen Miller will be
        a real bird.

Beautiful Snacks
Two mirrors feed each other yogurt,
Two mirrors feed each other shark.
Two mirrors lie on their backs.
Sun bounces off their chests.

Two mirrors don't want to move
But vow to follow one another.
Two mirrors exchange their silver
  backs and glass

      Two mirrors melt into each other.
      Two mirrors swim through caves,
      doing a lively breaststroke.

    They throw dirt
  on each other's shoes
    to get through the night.

Two mirrors wash each other
    and anoint the soles of
      their feet.
Two mirrors face each
  other and holler

into endless space.
Two mirrors argue
    as all mirrors do.

    They weep isolated solitude.
They vibrate within one another's light.

Wilda Morris
United States

After I Argued with Francisco during Dinner in San Miguel de Allende and He Dropped Something into My Diet Coke

My eyelashes fluttered, became butterflies,
cerulean and gold. They smelled like blueberries
so I plucked and ate them. The tortilla
I dropped tattooed a Mayan sun disk on my right ankle.
Drops of my blood splattered on the stripped floor,
became notes on a treble clef and sang La Bomba.
I leapt up, clicked my knuckles like castanets.
My blue jeans became a scarlet skirt.
I spun out into the night to the rhythm
of a painting by Frieda Kahlo,
whirled into El Jardin.

When I paid a pigeon cinco pesos
for three boxes of Clorets, it offered me wings
instead. I flew into the tower of La Parroquia,
pulled the ropes of all four bells. They were heavy
as Diego Rivera. When the bells rang, I jumped
onto the horse behind General Allende,
circling the park in his blue uniform.
Startled, the horse galloped fast
as the bite of a jalapeño. Francisco's laugh,
an octave higher than bougainvillea,
turned his cigarette into a stick, his teeth,
to corn-on-the-cob. I smeared butter
and chili powder on them and sold his mouth
in the north-east corner of El Jardin.

I clapped. Skin dropped off my arms and legs.

My face became a candy skull. I hobbled home alone,
now a Katrina on skeletal feet.

Tim Murphy
Spain

In a Mountain Dream
In a mountain dream
I am by the blue mountain.
It is morning and I feel the cool mountain wind.
I seek the river, but I am lost.
A woman walks down from the mountain.
I greet her and ask her where the river is.
Instead of answering she tells me her name is Nadja.
I am named after the book, she says.
In the distance I see the blue mountain
because now I am with Nadja by the river,
walking in sunlight, listening to the buzz of insects.
The past remains up for grabs, she says,
including more than the light, the water, and the matter.
Speaking of water, she adds, have you had enough
of the river? Yes, I say, and I explain
my feelings about mountains.
I understand, she says. Then I am with her
by the blue mountain again.
Now I know where the river is,
now the breeze is warm and gentle.
Nadja is trying to catch a butterfly with a net.
And something else, she shouts, laughing:
There are accidental encounters
tramped all over the rules of the game.

David Nadeau
Canada

Dark Healer Dream
The lion, at his decline, conjures the crossing of the fluids
The eyelids of clay are intoxicated
thunderstorms locked in small pebbles
the inexplicable sand of certainties
the snakes' sudden mathematics
the miniature wandering of the tribes and trumpets
The strange nodes of the dead, and the stairs, abound over
         ravines: the silverware of the fraudulent errors
The house appears
The parchment is rooted under the walls of the equinox
The inner fortress of the peacock declares its vow and its scarf
Humanity is the orthodox result of a deterioration in the
         syntax

The moon with spoon eyes turns against the brains
It sits in the fallen and rimless fire
the misshapen triangle of the angel

The metallic depths of the witchery immolate the entranced
         family
The pharmaceutical birth of the rectangle is wearing arterie
The ridiculous wind is a pestilential remedy
the pungent smoke of the unconscious treasure
The imperial neck reaches hypnosis
the profane boat of nail clippings
A sleepwalking planet predicts the bloodstained plagiarism
The tattooed bird threatens the Christian zodiac, code hatched
         in the eagle ingested by a consciousness
The royal egg accelerates
The flame breaks the mirror of asceticism
The ankle is a key coffin
The animal in ecstasy between two bites
dark healer dream

KB Nelson
Canada

Unspoken Words
3. You feel a full moon in a windowless room. You feel a full moon on a foggy morning. Hermit crab feels a full moon, as do earthworm, ant. Over-thinking makes the moon go away, be careful.

7. On the road today I see, apropos of nothing, a mashed cabbage. In the yard beside, a dog collar cone, the kind you get at the vet so they won't rip out their stitches. You, with your indigo lips and swaying skirt watch a little girl play bouncy ball five six seven. Ants follow their highway up the sides of the office building, like children who compete on sports day, all so invested in meaningless wins as grown-ups shield them from sunstroke and try to engage in conversation the little girl who smells like pee.

5. You walk among the tall thin pillars, drift around the triangles, touch the soft enamelled surfaces, curious fingers feel the imperceptible joins between layers of white and black and yellow. Calm, very calm, you move slow to the next, smooth and shiny. You're tempted to lick one. The light is soft easy, your feet are in milk, music so quiet you think you can't hear it. There are no circles.

1. Sometimes I speak in pastels. My friends and my family expect red arbutus or shadows to fall from my mouth but I like to change it up. They tell me persimmons, I reply cotton candy.

Kathryn Nocerino
United States

Flouncing Towards Havana
Carmen Miranda in Havana: a movie.
  her dancing-outfits were constructed by a
very great engineer
    out on a toot.
wash cycle in a launderette,

197

her hips rotate colors which clash
            harmoniously.

Carmen Miranda in Havana: a movie.
  free-floating vivacity
wilts the zoot suits of the gigolos.
  Cesar Romero disappears behind potted palms.
singed by the heat of this terrific orb,
  all of their minds have apparently become unhinged:
at the slightest persuasion, they burst into melody:
  paeans to the coconuts and brown-eyed burros.
pretty soon, everyone is speaking in patois:
  the owner of the largest cabaret in town;
the Fuller Brush man in from Pittsburgh, on vacation.

  this iron triviality cannot persist;
the pace is maddening.
  one by one they drop from sight into the canefields;
the khaki uniforms they wear are restful to the eyes.

Ciaran O'Driscoll
Ireland

Angel Hour
This morning I thought of the angels
I saw in a pre-dinner catnap
some years ago in Istria
and the tremendous crack
of thunder that same day
in a village where we lunched
on our way back to the coast.
I remember how they stood
in rank with their backs to me
on a road of golden clouds
that climbed into the sky
from our holiday bedroom.
Luminous, light as whispers,
I fancy they appeared
at the equidistant point

between lunch and dinner,
and wonder was that the point
of fasting in the old
church – vision's possibility,
the deeds of saints and martyrs,
the heights of Alvernia,
the desert and the voice
that cried in the wilderness?
The dry thunderclap
started me from my soup:
what I'd read about the war
came to mind though it never got
to the bistro we sat outside
on the borgo's single street.
I had ordered a second glass
of Pinot Grigio when bang!
a mortar shell behind me
blasted the afternoon.
But everything was OK,
the thunder merely a warning –
two glasses are enough –
and then the angels showed
in the stretch of abstinence
before the night's renewal
of appetite and glut

The Threshold of Quiet
He had arrived at the Threshold of Quiet
but hadn't crossed it. For a while he thought
about crossing, and felt he really should
now that he had arrived, but he didn't go:
something in his make-up wouldn't let him
cross the Threshold of Quiet. He wondered
what it was in his make-up that caused him
to stand there dithering and not go over.
He was still standing when a policeman
came up and said, "I am the Officer
of the Threshold of Quiet, and as for you,
it behoves you either to cross the Threshold
or go back where you came from. If you stand

199

much longer on the Threshold undecided,
I will arrest and caution you and then,
once cautioned and arrested, you'll be brought
to a place that you will definitely dislike
and you'll dislike it so intensely that
you'll wish you had gone over the Threshold,
or else headed back home. So now, me lad,
it's make-your-mind-up time, you can't stand there,
moping forever on the Threshold of Quiet.
I'm told that some regretted going back
the way they came, and that's all I can say.
It's not given me to tell you what's beyond.
If there was a way of going to that place
and sending word about it over here,
by now we'd surely know. You must decide."
Suddenly the pilgrim found his voice:
"Do you know what? I'd kill a cup of coffee."
The Officer scratched his head. "I suppose
I could let you have one if it's a help
in making up your mind. I have a jar
of instant in my hut." "Oh for God's sake,
forget it. I haven't travelled all this way
for instant slop." A fit of pique propelled
the pilgrim over the Threshold of Quiet
and quietness closed on him inexorably.

Head
(Los Cristianos, Tenerife)
There's a head on the water. I see it
every morning and evening as I stand
on the beach's frothy edge – the walrus head
of a healthy human specimen between
me and the motor-driven schooners moored
in mid-harbour, their sails superfluous
and furled; between the open sea
and the cactus-clustered mountains.

Between me on the hissing hem of froth
and the schooners' supernumerary sails,
between the cliffs and the promenade I see

200

a regular middle-aged humanoid head,
a brine-encompassed brainbox that proceeds
stealthily from my waking to my sleep,
its wet mouth lapped by whiskers, half-closed eyes
rapt in some indecipherable bliss.
A head that has made this incongruous
element its own, a head on its own
that has made the sea its own, a head
that I cannot get out of my own head,
moving without making sense between
the harbour mouth and the holiday apartments,
de facto as the cactus plants that rest
snug in their places on the mountain slopes.

I watch it daily from the ocean's edge
shifting without a ripple or a wake
in the lagoon between a reef of boats
and my reluctant water-testing toes,
I see it floating through recurrent dreams –
a king in a country of his own making,
capo di capi not to be discounted
in the fortunate isles of imagination.

A cranium building a head of steam
in its unwimpling progress up and down
the smoothness of the surface, unconcerned
by what is happening offshore or on.
This head of heads, no other head's contentment,
content without companion head, ensconced
in isolated mindfulness. A head
to end all heads, the mother of all heads.

Psyche
It was raining softly in the night
it was raining beautifully
I wanted to be at ease
enjoy the mist on my face
I also badly needed a leak
The Psyche was on her way
and Quintus texted me non-stop

about the terms of a bailout
Wheeling the rubbish bin
to the bottom of the cul-de-sac
I was plagued by lists of things to do
and the names of overly humble saints

Is there a word for this
the days that flutter by
in a gaggle of imperatives
the insistence of bodily functions
From grappling with the rose bush
my wrist is a night sky
and of course I'd prefer to lionize life
than write implicitly of death
or be the Sybil in a jar –
something must give the heart a lift
like the cool droplets on my face
even a touch of sympathy
to cry Freedom with the peoples
of North Africa
rather than agitate myself
in a stour of drudgery

With Quintus in his fervour
asking how Surrey are my suburbs
how London is my field
of vision for the futures
I have become more conscious
of the minutes measured out
only the daily assurance
of my androgynous beauty
in the mirror keeps me sane
still thinking how unlikely
the inevitable is

The Psyche is on her way
having climbed into the saddle
ages ago – it was the most
momentous fact of human life
that she had journeyed out at all

but sometimes nothing happens
for centuries and then
a century happens in a week,
and that's the Psyche's style –
to take her time about becoming
the unconquerable self

Seven times counter-clockwise
we jogged round the Chanctonbury Ring
and the Devil appeared to us
in a designer tracksuit
offering a broth of a bailout
liquidity support
a prohibitive interest rate
in exchange for our souls
Quintus said Yes and I said No
and I had to smile my best
androgynous smile at him
before he changed his mind
and the Devil disappeared
in a plume of shag tobacco smoke

And the word was made sex
as the flesh fell away from me
when I went on a paleo diet
and Quintus wrote me love poems
which only served to mask
the full extent of the deficit
I was sick from eating berries
in need of my stirabout
as if I had been waiting
for the dawn of agriculture

But the indestructible one
has climbed into the saddle
the Psyche is surely on her way
Even if the world implodes
she remains intact, entire
a rider over the ruins
of every incongruous thing

Or that's what I like to think
when I think of North Africa
and the constellations on my wrist
after my skirmish with the roses

Gloss

> It was evening all afternoon.
> It was snowing
> And it was going to snow.
> The blackbird sat
> in the cedar limbs. – Wallace Stevens

The blackbird is the place within you
which events cannot reach,
like a sound sleep this place
is without coming or going
and yet remains in touch
with everything that matters

I cannot really describe this place
of course it's not a place at all
how can a blackbird be a place?
the blackbird is in a place
among the cedar limbs,
and is simultaneously
a symbol and a blackbird

(Keep going)

Working on our house
a builder's labourer discovered
a bird's nest under the eaves
in a rusty gutter
The bird's nest is a bird's nest
and also a symbol for the heart

'Soul' is an ugly word,
it has been overused
to the point of extinction,
'Heart' isn't far behind,

it is better to speak of the blackbird
in the cedar limbs

'Love' has the same problem
as 'Soul' and 'Heart'
And if it hadn't been for the snow
and the cedar limbs, and the evening
which lasted all afternoon
the blackbird in strophe thirteen
might as well have been a magpie

(Keep going)

I don't want to keep going
because I don't think I can put it
clearer than Wallace Stevens
I could bring Zen down on you
or the Tao, hit you
with an Upanishad,
but you should be reading more,
meditating more
what's the point of me telling you
when you're not disposed
to get the point?

And when I say you I mean me
and when I say me I mean me
and which me, if any,
is the blackbird?
Is there a blackbird in me at all?
Is there a bird's nest under my eaves?

There have, indeed, been infinite bird's nests
and a lot of them are under eaves,
and not a few are in rusty gutters
and discovered by builder's labourers,
and it's easy to talk the talk
but to walk the walk that leads
to the place within
which is not a place at all

or even a blackbird
is a very different matter

(Keep going)

And love has been known to exist
without its name,
it has been known to get on fine
without its name
or any other name,
as for the soul, I have issues
and while 'Psyche' is too Greek –
beware the Greeks bearing gifts –
I have to admit 'The Psyche sat
in the cedar limbs'
has a certain ring to it

(Finish up now)

The blackbird was waiting
for the poet to finish writing
and the prospect of crumbs
from his evening-afternoon tea
The Psyche was waiting
for the poet to put the blackbird
sitting in the cedar limbs.

John Olson
United States

A Diamond in the Mind

It has often been my opinion that the color pink leads to metal detectors,
ultrasound, psilocybin, peyote, and Percy Bysshe Shelley. The romantic
spirit isn't dead. It's standing right there on a stepladder. Installing a
simulacrum. Something like Egypt. Would you like anything? A glass of
water? You've come this far. You can call an Uber if you want. That's the
end of the sentence. But it's not the end of the story. The story needs fire.
What is desired, what is most needed right now, is an art that smells of

sacrifice. All sweet things that come from the air merit the dance of paregoric, the blood around the bone murmuring softly like coal in the pursuit of beauty. There's beauty in dishevelment, beauty in punctuation, and beauty in light, but does Daylight Saving Time really matter, or is it just malarkey, a fruitcake feeding on lilacs? Matter doesn't always matter. Not when it's fluid. And there's a strange music in the air, teeming with qualia. That's when matter becomes a matter of experience, of essays, copulas, and process. Intensities mingling to create a momentum of unicorns & broccoli, chimeras stitched by hand. It feels good, that sudden contrast between the coldness of a glass of water handed to someone and the warm of their fingers. And this makes me undressed. Naked as a description. The poems of Emily Dickinson may be found in the glove compartment of my thumb. But nothing can replace nothingness like nothingness, or fill the hole in a lie with another lie. Redolence is not always red but the lips are supple when they find a purpose to what they say. So here. Have that glass of water. Glass & water provide impetus & context, but the water cannot be contained: the water is wild. It carries things away in the current. Squirts from a hose, sprawls into bayous, & roars as it falls from an edge of rock & plummets into the river below, the mad foam of the mind, in which it floats, and together become waves and eddies, each particular, each peripheral swirl.

If you compress a body of words hard enough with your mind, your concentration and focus, will it produce a diamond? What kind of writing would that be? What would it be called? And would it even matter in a postliterate world? Always keep a diamond in your mind, said Solomon Burke. Not sure what he meant by that. But I like the idea of it. The idea of it glitters. The idea of it is multifaceted, if poorly understood. If I shake my head can I hear it rattle? How much could I get for it? I don't think that's what Burke meant. Who once stopped a tour bus by a mortuary because his band didn't believe he'd once been a mortician. So they followed him into the mortuary and he showed them how it's done. It's done with great patience & care. There's your diamond. Think of it: the hardness of life, but also its maddening distinctions, its fluted bottles & newspapers. If you ask me mysticism smells of semantic shellac. Some things are transparent & some things are more like the soughing of willow. That's why I'm laughing at the road. It's so adorably hypnotic.

Nothing To Get Hung About

Optimism is hard to sustain in a world gone mad. Despair is easier. How is hope even possible? Hope is over. Forget hope. Hope makes things heroin. The rhythms are fat, like units of mechanical power, & tight as skin. Once everything gels, the day begins to boil, & the narrative arc of our lives get wrinklier & awkward. I can barely stand coherence anymore. It's goofy to fuss over feelings. They never make any sense. Words are insects, a dung beetle singing alone by a psychiatrist. When was the last time you sat at a small wooden table covered in oilcloth and thought about the humbleness of legs? And then bent down and picked up a jet-propelled reason for everything. What if meaning were a bunch of beans wrapped in a sound like a tasty tortilla? What if your ears jumped off your head & went swimming in some nearby music while you slobbered over a bean burrito? I feel the exultation of stone. This happened once in a dream & another time in the open where the words appeared to carry it away in a circus. No gun is truly cosmetic & the grammar is sad. Meaning is hard to find when it's sewing itself up with rain. It is not my objective to be obvious. We all want liposuction. But how many among us are willing to renew the moonlight in our minds with a seemly seme and a seamstress? Wave your hand. I think that's our taxi. Now sit down. I want to tell you something. Nouns are knots. Periscopes. Knockers. We occupy a world connected by hearing and smelling and tasting and sight, images that gleam in the sun like dragonflies, regrets and memories that create a landscape of willows and brooding clouds. The trick is to never hit the ground. Today I feel a little hypnosis around me. My underwear helps me understand spitting oatmeal at the windshield. Most religions travel at an average speed of reverie, which is a daydream of everything sordid and poor becoming blessed, John Lee Hooker dancing across the stage in a Brooks Brothers suit and a bowler hat, shooting lightning out of his guitar. Knowing how to vary the language we use and the narratives we create would be a way of approaching the complexity of reality by escaping binary logics, to the point of accepting the coexistence of opposites in the world and in oneself. To understand it, must we experience it as a revelation. Or can we just buy a gun & shoot it? If the imagery of war enters here, it's fake. I've never been to war. Never fired a machine gun. Never threw a grenade. My war has been fought silently in rooms. The war of the imagination, as di Prima described it, "the war that matters is the war against the imagination / all other wars are subsumed in it," and I believe this is true. When there is rage in a populace just below the surface, graffiti on closed up stores and people living in tents, there's been a war. A very evident war. Mass shootings. Shock. Disorientation. Women walking down streets without pants. Smartphone zombies in a trance. When was the last time you thought something contrary, something unpopular, something full of rage & suspicion, something destructive, something negative, & held back, because there was a smartphone in the room, or a laptop, or a PC, &

they have microphones, even on or off they can't be trusted with your privacy, & so you held back, said nothing, or diluted it a little, made it a little more acceptable, adorned it with qualifiers and rationalizations & made it a little blurry, a little equivocal, just a squib, a carefully edited tweet, & felt diminished, a little less alive? I think it's time to start talking about Umwelt, semantic blobs of nothingness. But don't overdo it. Don't swallow the universe. Concentrate on dopey Joey's aioli. And nothing to get hung about.

Crazy Patterns On My Sheets

Good to see a motel, even if you don't plan on stopping & checking in. It's nice to know it's there. It provides a way out of all the unnatural concerns with one's well-being. When life ceases to be a faked wrestling match & assumes the grandeur of trout we must solicit the gods & drink extra amounts of coffee. Consciousness is a boulevard of boundless dahlia. You'll find ice cubes in the freezer, epiphanies in beans. Dexterity like this isn't natural, but it leads to enchantment, & fine stationary. When you understand your mind in this way, there'll be a big fat pillow, & boats at night. Lie back. Imagination is what happens when ripples move to the shore in Shakespeare's sonnet, each changing place with that which goes before, & getting your mind wet. Moisture is a function of soliloquy. I get quiet in the bathroom. I'm a Dickens in a duck suit. I'm a geyser of spiders & a friend to the web. I'm a crease of Keats & a sign of Stein. I like phosphorus hats multipurpose knives & long walks on the beach. But enough about me. Let's talk about you. You is a pronoun, I know, but I also knew the prepositions that helped bring you into being. It took a lot of lifting. Pumping. Heavy breathing. It took a team of crack cartoonists just to draw your nose. But hey, I dig your overall look. I like the uniformity of plaid & the flow of your tie is nothing less than suave. The eyeball gloves & intestinal sweater are quietly understated. Gold lamé seems a little too flashy these days, as things often do post-Presley, but you learn to accept this, because chickens have the mass of bears when the weather permits, & their feathers are soft as fog. Funny to think I've gone my entire life without wearing a uniform. I guess my old hippie clothes were a strange species of uniform, though they were far from uniform, they were pluriform, a miscellany of items collected, on the sly, from museums & theatres, a brocaded caftan with gold buttons, doublet, codpiece, frogging, jerkin, passementerie, & a Spanish cape of orange velvet. These days all I really want is a simple theater & a little knot in my brain to come undone. Do I belong to the wind? Nobody belongs to the wind. I cherish these hours of bee palpation. Is it archaic to believe the moon drools virgins? Birth has an answer. The good kind, with periscopes and introspection. Most religions travel at an average speed of reverie, which is a daydream of *darshan*, which is Sanskrit for viewing, or point of view, and is the act of beholding a deity, a revered person, or sacred object. Everything else is just sprinkles on a sundae. Therefore, the golden jelly of vision enters its articulation & feels the warm dreams of earth under the eyelid of night. There will come a time & it will howl a language nobody understands. It will sound like silk & carry its own reasoning. It will sound like something near and far, and have the sweetness of berries, & blow onto land like the morning mist, & harden into words.

Swizzle Stick Physics

I wish I could reach out and grab time and pull it back and keep it from moving so damn fast. I feel like I'm sitting in the cockpit of a formula one car on a highway toward a fatal destination. No U turns. No exits. I'm not even driving the car. I don't know who or what is driving the car. I'm just a passenger. I don't even have a map. Or a spare tire. Don't get me wrong. I think the universe is pretty. But it's moving too fast. I want to sit by the side of the road & read a map. Or Jack Spicer. Is there a Jack Spicer Atlas? Where are we, Jack? "Be there / Like the earth / When shadow touches the wet grass." How beautiful that there is such flux in the universe. Skates and glamour and heraldry. Time isn't just so much gobbledygook. It has a pattern. Infancy is being seated at a table, childhood is the aperitif, adolescence is a trip to the rest room, adulthood is the main course, late middle-age is the desert, and old age is the bill. And here I stand on a March afternoon, a glass in one hand, sponge in the other, as I do the dishes, and attune myself to what is at hand. Click of the plastic Ocean Spray Cran-Cherry bottle after I stomped on it, reducing its volume before tossing it into the recycling bag. The bottle returns to its original shape. Or tries to. Reminds me of an afternoon in a hotel cocktail lounge with my father and him gazing at a swizzle stick and bending it and telling me plastic has a memory as the stick resumed its original shape. Form is emptiness, emptiness is form, say the Buddhists. Open a photon, and what do you see? Energy oscillating in waves. Dark energy. Dark matter. Antimatter. What an ancient hole. This shiny black imaginary cave. Right there, under your skin, is a bonanza of art. I think of feeling things as an art in & of itself, especially when a machine can do anything if it's monotonous enough. Sometimes I want to tell a sausage something & then I forget & say to myself oh for crying out loud I smell existence. One day you're writing so many ideas that they bang around in your skull like a maraca on meth & the next day there are horses. That's pretty good. Thank you, language. Thank you for consciousness, lumberyards & fog. The lighthouses have been displaced by modern technology but the shores remain the same, water whispering into the sand, making rhetoric on a rock. It's winter. The sky speaks to us with traffic lights & spaceships. Welcome to Planet Earth. It's really great here. We've got elephants, savannahs & Bluetooth. We listen to podcasts. Queen Mab discusses glittery human skulls & Denmark with an expert on crustaceans. I'm feeling insolent in my ramifications. I've been here a long time. Life here is blunt & complex. Even the pancakes are served nervously. Self-awareness is experienced with words. This led me to write with .38 caliber Smith & Wesson. I'm hooked on polyphony. The ricochets go better with prose. But the games are played with jigsaws, our drinks are stirred with swizzle sticks, which make the equations tremble, & grow into thunder.

The Stay-At-Home Astronaut Manual
What would happen if the universe burped? Maybe it has burped. Maybe it burps all the time. Maybe there wasn't a big bang. Maybe there was a big burp. This is known as the burp theory. Theories are burps of intellect. They occur after eating hypotheses. Hypotheses are delicious. They taste like chicken. Everything I've experienced in life has either been a complete surprise (most of it has been a complete surprise) or a disappointment. There have been a lot of disappointments. The ratio of appointments to disappointments is pretty thin. I don't want to sound non-committal, but when I close my eyes I drift away into the magic night. This is how I discovered England. It came to me packaged as chocolates. No wall is impenetrable, but some people want to make you believe that they're bulletproof. I don't know why they insist so much on this. Today's literature would rather fool around with the faculty than learn the ukulele. I feel present. That's what's important. Being there. It's crucial. You've got to get up and ask someone to dance eventually. Otherwise what's the point? You've got to invent a narrative for yourself. Me, I'm still working on it. It's too late to become an astronaut. At least in the orthodox sense, with a helmet, a paycheck and a degree in aeronautics. I'm more the stay-at-home kind. I'm already in space. What else are you going to call this space around me? I call it a room. It's got a view. But not it's not in the window. It's in my head. Which has windows called eyes. Which I require for space travel. Inertia works well as well. I like to lie in the bed watching the stars behind my eyes. Think of it. About 100 trillion neutrinos pass through your body every second. How does that make you feel? It makes me feel transparent as the wings of the dragonfly. It makes me feel ephemeral. Blissfully ephemeral. And sad. There was no meaning in the end. No apparent

meaning. There were the meanings we created. But did that confer them with any reality? Meaning requires testimony. Meaning requires a steady framework. A context. A norm. A dispersal. Meaning is pollen. Poets are bees. They be bees. You can feel it in their sting. Where does that come from? There's an ocean in every human being and no one can reach the bottom. The basis of the universe may not be energy or matter but dog collars. If you don't believe me, try whistling. See what comes. Remember Walter Huston laughing his head off at the end *of Treasure of the Sierra Madre* when all that gold dust blows away in the wind? I think Kierkegaard would've like that. You've got to learn to trust your brothers and sisters in space. Not their bank accounts. Space travel promotes camaraderie. It's cold in space. The baseline temperature of outer space, as set by the background radiation from the Big Burp, is -454.81 degrees Fahrenheit. Bring a sweater.

Bart Plantenga
Netherlands

List: 1984 Jersey Coast Observed
nudie mags bottom of the pile, junk store
scurrilous books
spike heels
panty lines / tan lines
smell of sweat and no. 30 in cracks
old drive-ins
writing about things that happen
skinny-dipping [10pm / don't scream to avoid detection
         by beach cops]
mushrooms
calm days with the smell of lilacs in the air
sex in field of tall grass with the sounds of bees buzzing
sex in the dunes after a long walk
sociological tour of Atlantic City [boring is the new
         thrilling]
ripped posters on walls
slurping the foam off a cappucino
strawberry daquiris [early]
late night walk on beach [cheap beer, sand on genitalia]
beach glass collected

heated discussion about movies with lots to drink
art doodles
intimate memoirs of writers read aloud
WFMU donate time
bad bad movies – 2 lists
about my own views and visions
smell of early rain on summer dust
buying flowers vs picking wild flowers
ferris wheels [nausea or vertigo?]
hugging an old friend
junk shops [4 pairs of Converse hi-tops $40 – red, green, light blue, black]
watching people walk by [people only walking to get to a
        car. why?]
meet interesting people
the idea to plagiarize their lives [for a while] performance
lick salt off back of her hand
[predict rent hike or demise]

Rochelle Potkar
India

Somna
I walk the trail of adolescent shadows
between wakefulness and sleep.
Primitive awakenings of my ancestors -
the Jekyll and Hyde of moon-types.

Drifting into other places like a con artist,
under blankets of theta waves in limbic sensing.
With gene-memory, a vortex of smudging trails
behind curtains of my cortex.

The night closes its lids on partial dangers,
the quivering of arrows, shooting like stars.

I lay awake even in orgasms. There are no latches on my doors.
The doors are in my head, unbolting the light in my nerve,

spotting darkly guns at trigger points.
Like migratory frigate birds
that fly for months in their sleep.
Behind shut eye, alert,
searching the dark stars through the third eye.
The rain in the abyss holds up summers
as secrets give in,
sheltering the unspooling of dress-rehearsals.
Survival of revivals.

A candle worth of hope upsets the trail
at the end of the tunnel,
as the morning moon gloats on sleeping pills,
musky odors of day dreams.

Not even the adultery of vodka works on my gut
in the upstream rivers of denial,
- sips of forgiveness metabolizing,
continuums of realization.
Prolonging the hindrances of surrender
to the shadows that pull
over the longitudes of night.

Orna Rav-Hon
Israel

Gleaning
I gathered your features in the field.
I set them down beside me.
Over head a white bird circled
your lightened sparks.

The Touch of Stars
Why is this wind telling me
these soothing words?
Just moments before
my body was not consumed
by fire

and it controls me now
like the burning bush
drawing from within my hands
the touch of stars.

Translated from the Hebrew by Karen Alkalay-Gut

Love Measure

Your hands in my body
establish their territory,
inspiring him
with beautiful spirit
until my body rises naked
from the cerements
staring at us
with its white bones.

Translated from the Hebrew with the author
by Stanley H. Barkan

Bronwyn Rodden
Australia

in English air
thundering horses over the stiles
the fragrant procession lost to summer light

past the angelica sea
a slim layer over delta sand

eased in bucketfuls
onto shelly grains shifting

settling themselves onto
a new shore

late into the ricketty darkness we ride
feeling the body inside

footfalls on lichened stones and heather
past the hiss of waves to the right

always keep the water to your right
we enter a flask of rainy forest

fern whelps splash the face
a fronded touch
static the space between oblivions
let's stay awhile

lift our feet to air
tongues to fire all full of scenery

stragglers sight the clearing of tents
fierce smoke and bacon pungent in night air

take down the canopy and we'd be
in the stars

wrestling with allegorical riddles
all the same days and days an answer?

the body inside pushes out a word
we took it for a wraith and led on

always opening our burnt mouths and
showing withered tongues grey with age

not hearing again the body inside
remembering

Addict
Sunday slabs the week again
wind death-white and hasty
cut the thread of responsibility
lay me with a voice of fiction
gimme a line

Stranded like a paw in milk
push it all outside again
joy-ride straight to heaven
who cares what the point is

gimme a line

Round the circle dragging
fifteen housemaids on their knees
push them through the windswill holes
paint them in your Rembrandt-ese
gimme a line
Hurtle down town into it
fleshy knives make stories stick
coloured scarlet, purple, white,
Tiger Tiger burning bright
gimme a line

Salutations on frosty moons
Catherine's calling for the bored
Dorothy scolds the sheep on track
Williams in the flowers again
gimme a line

Star knight star bright
hit me with it curled up tight
cut and hack no-ones listening
do it slowly in your kitchen
gimme a line

Find a mountain top
mountain crater,
mountain lake
mountain monk
mountaineer
mountain devil
mountain eyrie way up high
gimme a line

Break Break Break all the
feet of your cane toads
oh see
touch the magic button
puff the magic pastry
gimme a line

Splatten satin sardine shoes
tip and touch and soon the bloom
overcame his gorgon fume
plays the Billy tailor-blue
gimme a line
gimme a line
all fall down

A singular plane, a moment
Light is dull on the outside stairs,
the yellow of cats' eyes on unfruitful nights,
a body repeats the arc of hand to banister
to head over and over.

There's no music in the alley
by the green-grey fence smelling of alders
it could be a picture in a gallery
with plastic floors and children hanging
tired from parents' hands
and one dull light to hide away the shadows
the noiseless night and the unseen alley.

It might be on TV, was it a repeat?
Perhaps it was American; skeletal stairs
clinging to a classic brownstone walkup:
categorisation as art.

But it could be an hotel.
It's dark and wherever it is, it's waiting
a scene of dull yellow tired yellow and darkness.
The person on the stair waits
is waiting for the scene to change
for it to make the first move.

The Moon, That Glistering Tear
And in the fifteenth century house
On the left side of the road
The woman sat for fifteen years
Amidst her dismal load

I'll do it now, she said and when
She went out to the porch
She noticed Micky with the cat
He'd turned into a torch.

Rod Carlos Rodriguez
United States

Rooting for Spices
Caciques live
in my heartbeat,
swim in my corpuscles,
drown in my brown skin,
and are reborn
in my voice.

Their rushing rivers
part my curls,
pour through my
open iris
at 3am,
filter my vision
in mimosa leaves, golden sunsets,
Utuado mountains,
and the Adjuntas pueblo.

Taino paint my breath
in tongues
murmured down to
my toes, my hands,
the edges of my criollo.
Mi gente de
Mayagüez, Bayamon,
and Cabo Rojo
keep feeding, caressing
these roots
fatigued by
a half millennium

fighting güeros, Spanish Crowns,
and the Caribe.

I hear el piratas
whispering through
taste buds
embracing oregano,
cilantro, Sazón
and the body follows,
joins, leads me deep
into El Yunque's forest,
by diamond emerald
shores,
of Boriken,
of home.

Salomé Waits
Beside Abacoa's river,
beneath Aruaca's
Cueva Ventana, she

caresses tobacco leaves,
gently presses them
between thumb and index finger.

Waits. As days, weeks,
decades coat the trail
back to his cave.

His promised kiss
remains moist on
her cohoba-laced lips.

Waits. Hours, months,
lifetimes season her belief
in Aruaca's return.

Even Yocahú rests
His hands on Salomé's
pale shoulders, whispers *patience*.

Waits. As coqui's cries serenade
behind last night's downpour.
Still angry at Don Julian's

rejection of Aruaca,
Salomé remains
unaware her lover

died at her father's
feet. She remains seated,
every night in Cueva Ventana.

Waits.

Bodega Lights
Don Pedro counts the change,
eighteen dollars and ninety-eight cents,
gently lands the coins
in Elizam Escobar's
callused, paint-smeared hands.
Revolution red
bright on his right pinky.

In the corner, by the rack
of notebooks and ASPIRA
literary primers,
Oscar Jose Lopez avoids
thoughts like sedition,
conspiracy, but mulls over letters
like F and A, L and N.

Dylcia Pagán quickly
enters la Bodega, her mind
on the next cause that
MENDs her activism with
commitments towards country,
the people, struggle,
and independentista of soul.

Lolita Lebrón stands atop

the boxes of White Castle burgers,
screaming at shoppers,
her luger and voice drowned out
by the slurpy machine,
dripping on the feculent tiles
dingy with stars and stripes.

Holding Lolita's ankles,
Rafael Cancel Miranda
And Irvin Flores Rodríguez
glare at other customers,
chins out, even as
Andres Figueroa Cordero
waves a tattered, Puerto Rican flag.

Behind the counter,
Pedro Albizu Campos stops
counting change and fires
up the gathered nacionales,
a radioactive halo
surrounds him in holy
testament to martyrs
of Isla Del Encanto.

Stuart Ross
Canada

The Parents All Cried
It was a quiet time for us.
A man with two heads lived in our garage.
The price of fuel was plummeting.
Mother had already collected
twenty miniature folksingers.
We hid beneath our desks
because a crow had gotten in.
Outside, a jalopy was idling.
The lights went out when
Velda, the janitor,

slammed the classroom door.
Our teacher's voice was soothing.
We lay on the floor on mats.
The radios began sputtering;
the televisions went black.
In St. Petersburg, explosions were heard.
We lifted our Barbies and Kens
and chewed the heads off our dolls.
The parents all cried
when the monkey bars fell. We
took the broken tricycle and
flung it into the canyon.

After Pierre Reverdy

Look,
only one alarm clock is left.
It rings. There is no one to read
the time. Even the rodents
are dead. The wind searches
for a leaf to twang. All is dark.
The earth no longer bothers
turning. What difference
would it make anyway?
Lakes and ravines can't
tell themselves apart.
The books are full of words
but what's a word?
The night disappears
with a breath.

Please Write This Down
after Barbara Guest

An egg gallops. It wears a ring, splashes into a pool of tangled syllables. The head of a sparrow replaces my own head, so we'll have enough time to share a marble tomato and dance among the nubile chairs of elsewhere.

Have you ever been lost in a forest? Have you ever escaped from a thieving potato field? Feel the brush of leaves across your brow, something cold across your dark and dignified throat. Have you ever used the word "apparatus" in a poem? I just did. And thus the poem smells.

Crawl into this careless, embittered bed, and gaze at the wall opposite, where a photograph is mounted of the president of Switzerland, pens hanging out of his nostrils. Little did we know that we would someday fling our watches—and our wrists—from the pebble-strewn road.

Please write this down. Write this down while giving me a look both contaminated and affectionate. All by yourself, you have invented the laboratory.

Now Showing
The crunch of popcorn faded.
The credits began rolling.
A rabbit chased an ostrich
in the open field.
They told me my name was Ed.
I threw a party
after my brother collapsed.
It was eleven forty-three.
Four wings were glued to my back.
Wonder all around me.
A boll weevil watched me from my untidy desk.
Beneath it I discovered
three sports cars and a duck.
I didn't know how to talk
as a result of phones hadn't yet been invented.
A window exploded.
Huge gusts of octopus
billowed out of my eyes.

My Years in Exile
They paid me $150,000 an episode to write a drama series about a hammer, a tadpole, and a Q-Tip.

This changed my life.

People rushed me on the streets, I lived in an airplane, I wore shirts made of celery and silk.

It's not like the work was easy.

The producers interfered with my scripts: "Make it more tawdry," they said.
"Give the hammer a busty girlfriend."
I clung to my principles and held these guys off as long as I could.

This was my art, after all.

But they destroy everything, these people, they put rock salt in your porridge,
they defrost your cat, they crawl all over your ham-laced running shoes.

In exile, I wore lavender robes and wrote autobiographies of Kim Novak.

Here it was winter year-round and we huddled by our woodstoves, playing card
games and telling jokes.

Television had not yet arrived, and no one knew that I had been the most
celebrated scriptwriter of the post–*My Mother the Car* era.

Oftentimes, while my family slept, I snow-shoed to the edge of town, to the
snow-swept fields of abandoned bathtubs, where I chose a tub and therein
crouched, singing fragments of my bar mitzvah *parsha*, whose words sailed into
the cold wind like chimney swifts startled by a clumsy bear.

Then I would pull myself to my feet,
and clap my wings against my body,
and the thunder was heard
across the nation.

Pauline Rowe
United Kingdom

Two Children Are Threatened by a Nightingale
after Max Ernst

Stolen from an ancient stage
we were fixed in the blue, my sister and I –

we do not believe in the low light
or whisperings of parents.

We were part of the scenery
for the Midsummer play.
There are no trees   just cerulean, green layers –
paint that sticks to my feet, imitating grass.

I am the body of the girl on the ground,
the one in his rescuer's arms, the girl with the knife.

At the vanishing point, in the bend, the end
of the city wall, there is a ghost palace, a marble arch.

The man on the roof has silver skin,
sings falsetto, clasps a child.

Perhaps his life or liberty depends on flight?

He reaches for the doorbell to escape the frame
but he can't reach, and the bell is a prop.

We cannot hide here now as it stands
in the ploughed-up blue, a sea of paint

yet the terracotta handmade life is standing
in the middle of your dream.

     Dear Loplop. Stop dying –
     open the small wooden door of the hut
     and I will hide there, lie on the dusty floor,

     breathe in spores and black soot,
     listen to superman on the roof.

I am wrapping your bones in paper, rubbing all
textured surfaces for patterns   with my teeth.

I cover everything with thin silk, try to find
what you had to tell me, scrape away your pigment.

There are eyes in the grain of wood
the frame becomes a beak that doesn't sing.

We know the catchers kept them
for the autumn lock-up.
The drive to migrate made them dash themselves
to death against the bars of the cage.
I am hungry for Christmas figs,
an open fire, dawn prayers.

Although it has flown upwards, dull bird of the scrubland,
I wish to kill the nightingale.

(Please don't tell anyone this.)

      Dear Loplop, please come back.

      Find your glass eye,
      climb out of your dust.

Lisa Samuels
New Zealand/United States

Everyone agrees and you have culture
The elect, morphemically engrossed
is beautiful, his haunch par terre
like the horsey appended to a carousel
whose figures of motion self-deceive.

'Safari,' he's telling me about it, one exquisite
fortitude after another. We purr on land
in grasses, on highways made of carpet
the pinks of funerary curiosity

Not that economy isn't the central basis of
blood terror, but the woman in the cake
knew how to get out of there fast
(he did it, he stayed right there in his doubt!)

They all smiled enormously their boundaries
lightened. After that, one might hope to *be thinking*.
Hyperions of crème brûlée, cities

one would heretofore have no reason to spell.

Anacoluthon
that's that island there and I am not the day recedes
the man standing in a memory of the man standing
if I had a temple to relax in, it would be almond trees
those abeyed above our heads with mild bitterness
leaves tired having sprung in the spell
the news is over before it can be called –
it's a way of paying attention, that's the ticket
I have governed for someone's sake though has it been –
and lovely are the grasses, lovely the spell, the limbs cast upward
tellingly, his little hands climb the air, purposeful
(and the youthful self he once was, lovely and externalized all
            nerves
and now embedded, imbued, re-tigered)
underneath the lemon tree all is forgiven
we suck until our voices ring like bells

Jeanie Sanders
United States

Without a Nose a Person Can't See Heaven
Little Egypt,
dancing under the shadow
of Abu Simbel
stumps her toe and
falls in pain.
As the men who beat rhythm
whirl faster.

Down she falls
cascading steel pointed stars
for breasts
molded to pierce
the dry earth.
The noise from her thighs
coming together
vibrates across

the shutter of Du Camp's camera.
Just as he lowers the black hood
to shut out light and
condemn man to an image.

Still farther on
the Great Sphinx turns his head
and is caught
in the slowly turning sound
of the aperture
breaking his nose off.

Steven Schroeder
United States

Not
Woke up dreaming the end of the world
this morning. You were on the phone asking
after the melting moon, whether one could
still swim in it. But sun is rising

faster than you can imagine
and going is slow everywhere
in this double viscosity. Meringue
clouds streaked orange, whatever

had been waiting to be born of it nothing
but embryonic weight spreading
to stop you, stop you breathing.
And in the end, I think not.

Fahredin Shehu
Kosovo

The White Flame
all those years this flame...
All those invisible burns

bruises and blisters
waiting to turn yellow
like the old Cypress of Abarukh
I stand winded by winds
of all colours and heat...
harsh rains and potent flashes hit mercilessly,
they even chopped
my boughs and twigs.

Yet this white flame of mine
mild the pain of
all those in sorrow
all these in despair
all those who got enkindled
by the blue flame of Love
by the green flame of the Divine
by the red flame of passion.

When you open my letter
I left under your pillow and
read the just words for the curved world...
all those words that shine and blind your vision

remember to:
spell the Code of Existence
letter by letter writing LOVE

remember too:
the harsh winters and
the hell- heat of the Balkan
confused summer

let your teardrop leak and
drop upon each letter
to fertilize it
to resurrect...
to enliven this Entity
that lost its way in the Universe
and fell upon my Heart
to emanate this White Flame

A Quantum Taste

She pulled up her dress,
the foot touching the water membrane,
the thrill currents from foot
                    to the head-top,
goose bombs on the skin all over,
a grape-berry in her mouth
foaming, burgundy drops-
                    leaking on her jaw.
Tasteful indeed- the wine to become,
as if all tastes disappeared
only for this moment of
Quantum reality I dwell and
the Time lost its meaning.

Marcus Slease

Spain / Ireland

Black Hole

I stepped inside the wooden restaurant. A hurly burly man came
to the dinner table. He was tall and also bearded. He took my girlfriend and
they had their way with each other. I cannot grow any taller I said. But I can
grow a beard. And thus began the beard growing. I have to shave my neck I
said. It gets too itchy. Fair enough she said. I have to shave around my lips I
said. I don't like hair in my mouth. Fair enough she said. Many years went by.
My beard was very long. I must have won. I was inside a log cabin. The log
cabin was in the hands of a small boy. I looked out of the log cabin. It was a
jungle of carpet. It was so thick. It must have been the seventies. Disco hits
were spinning somewhere in another room. And thus I began my journey with
a plastic knife. I hacked my way through the carpet. It was very itchy. I
reached the kitchen. My beard trailing along the ground. Where do I come
from? Where am I going? Why am I here? The universe has an ancestor.
Another universe. Born inside a black hole. The universe reproduces with
black holes. No black holes means no reproduction. You need a black hole.
Where is your black hole? Only survival of the fittest. Black holes. I must
find my black hole I said. I climbed the cupboard and reached a very bulky
microwave. I stepped inside. The radio waves whooshed. Ding. I woke up
inside an 80's microwave. It was smaller. The radio waves whooshed. Ding. I

231

woke up inside a millennium microwave. The microwaves were getting smaller. They were evolving. The big bang is now the big bounce. The universe is a wave. The universe is a string theory. An unexplained patch of nothing in cosmic microwave background radiation. I stepped back inside. I bounced around. I was a real human.

Lawrence R. Smith
United States

Monkey in the Moonlight, With Birds
Psycho-bop monkey, his tail a dactyl that
inscribes a name, takes us back where
nerves enter spine, and look who's a hero now.

You can't change your bones underwater. This he
knew, but in his brief and hungry moods birds
appeared on the rusty wire of delicate branches.

The wind rang the temple bell and the clatter
of jackdaws sounded like his mother singing.
Is this fractured moon a curtain or a wing?

Birds are scraps or rags snagged on the wire,
then clean gone like flowers in the dark,
like the intelligence of a turning tide.

*   *   *

Monkey recited his Book of Chores, the seams
of his galoshes fluent in the moonlight.
Let birds make footprints on dissonant clouds.
He knew them by name, plugs in the birth of air,
solar winds that fondle even in the dark:
snapshots, swimming lessons in the ark of history.

Second Sight
The river call, with its vague profile
for seeding all paths to sight:
find a tiny fire behind her eye
as it is razor-carved in moonglow.

The tattoo on her back is an open quest:
ink rises above the skin, seeds
its own battle, an infantry of feet,
hands, and eyes.

Outside the skull, inside flame's canyon,
loud in all its edges, the end of ease,
a floating rose, nirvana.

John Snelling
United Kindom

Roads to Freedom
Some have gone directly, leaving their luggage
They will find only a drunken octopus.
Those who have walked three times in the winding ways
Must nurse the glass baby.
O long is the way and far, but we who ride
The fleet foot camels of eternity
Shall not be troubled by the wandering bone.

Fantasy
In the ancient town of Cirencester
There is concealed a strange little restaurant
Where dinners are served that run on wheels
And the ovens are powered by electric eels,
Where the lights are bright green
And the waiters are swans
Where the walls are of glass
And the tables of bronze,
Where the finest of truffles are twopence a pound,
But don't try to find it
For it cannot be found.
This unreachable place, like all else of its sort, is
But a dream in the night of the singing tortoise.

Interim Police Report on Samuel Taylor Coleridge

Coleridge: Samuel Taylor   Male   IC1   date of birth: 21/10/1772

I identified the suspect by his flashing eyes and floating hair.
Typical signs of a poet.

Forensic analysis of his body fluids disclosed
traces of honeydew and milk of paradise.

Documents seized from his premises indicate
that his supplier is one Khan – Kubla.
Islamic?

Among his associates is an Abyssinian maid.
Musician, apparently.
Also an un-named woman with a demon lover,
known to haunt savage, holy and enchanted places.
May be identified by her habit of wailing.

Suggest liaison with the River Police
to identify the organisation's runner, Alf.

Suspect to continue to be held for questioning by the Wildlife Unit
in connection with the deranged old sailor
currently in custody for killing an albatross,
possession of an offensive weapon
and harassment of passers-by.

The Golems

We are of clay and earth and spit and slime.
We execute a script placed in our heads,
obey our orders, cannot deviate.
We feel nothing.
We work.
Our tools are hammers, spades,
our tools, our weapons.

Builders and breakers of walls we are
inexorable as a landslide.

Relentless, dense, no fence
nor boundary contains us.
Behind us they lie broken.
We work, we fight,
we build, we destroy.

We go on.
You made us.
Be afraid of us.
We stop for nothing,
certainly not for you.

Sou Vai Keng
Portugal / Macau

a moon of my own
i draw a circle and travel with it to the moon
someone has drawn in the sky another moon
and another and another and some have named them
moon more often than not distracted by others
with love and fear and sometimes
forget there is always their own moon

i draw a circle with lines round and round
the wind seems to lead the clouds clouds
seem to know where to go on the way home yet
never reaching home perhaps we are
moons too far away the way we are
drawn to each other and apart

i draw a circle and carry the moon everywhere
i go inside is all i have do not have
i take out all i want to give and take
but it is you i will always keep in this
never-ending round and round we travel
until we lose track of time time travels

i draw a circle in red red makes you think of the sun
and believe it is hot where i am not where my body is
you so far away my friend like the mud yellow desert
i draw with a sliver of blue the moon hidden behind gray clouds
you the body only shell of a longing for
the reds of a moon soul can travel with

Dancing on a crossing

On a half painted zebra crossing Maria's tender feet skip over black and
white, body slithering through lights of morning sun, like a charmed snake,
dancing to a music no human hand can play; Dona da Pina stooping on her
walking stick at the curb, standing still, chants lyrics to be seen by eyes good
at reading lines between and beyond; burdened minds rush by, hurrying to
some kind of destination that they stubbornly believe exists.

At the end or middle of the slippery zone of humankind, Maria touches the
last black stripe with both hands, feet stretching far to the edge of a free
world, belly towards sky, arching over to form a rainbow on which will walk
those who dare look life in the face; Pina steps on the first white stripe and
stops short, lost in thought or in action before a misty chaos, circling round
and round like a secret elixir a witch is stirring.

As Pina moves slowly to the end or the middle of the crossing knowing
nobody knows where the end is, knowing nobody will have to cross and
finish the walk, four impatient artificial feet rush through under Maria's
bridge and screech to a standstill. Everybody stops to look, but nobody can
see a zebra flying, carrying two defiant angels, wild and uncontained,
wrestling bravely with time in front of the entrance or exit of our space.

so naked, you see nothing
you are so naked
i cannot see anything

i put your flesh into my mouth
and swallow the sounds of an ocean

it is love i hear
when you die

it is death i face
when i am alive

i am so naked
you see nothing

Ruth Stacey
United Kingdom

*

Reveries, the wall is green. A door leads to our past lives, so we keep it locked; I peep
through when everyone else is in bed. So beautiful! Such fun! It is a land of hills and
rivers. A woman is on stage. Her bodice is trimmed with ermine and her skirts are
embroidered with red tulips. On her wrist, a hooded falcon. How it pulls to get away!
The woman loves her spirited falcon, she strokes it tenderly. The jesses are fitted with
copper bells. They chime and I wake. Edy floats through the hallways; her nightgown
is sky-blue cotton. I kneel to see how her magic works. Edy, I say, what are you
reaching for her? Her fingers make the shape of a bull. My hair is curled into buns held
in place by orange flowers that were grown for the wives of sultans. Edy issues an
edict.

*

Over the rim of the cup I see bronze feathers.
An angel is waiting for a steak cooked
bloody in the middle. I will cook it
when I have poured my drink.
The meat waits on the table,
bleeding on the plate.

An angel's hum is just out of human hearing—
an insatiable pause between lightning and strike.
Grating the spice, and stirring, takes aeons. He sighs.
In the armchair, the magnificent legs fidget,
cramped wings tremble. There is no heartbeat.

I smile; he will wait whatever the discomfort.
One feather falls onto the rug, its curved barbs
submissive, asking to be stroked.

The spiced milk is warm, and I pour. The angel
reaches over and turns over the cup, no liquid
falls. He smirks, *a parlour trick*. Dove-light,
it slips down the throat. After this, nothing will sate.

Wally Swist
United States

Dream of Judita Vaiciunaite
In the dream, she arranges to meet me aboard the cutter.
Our hair streams in the wind, and I ask her about the women

Sitting upon the rocks of the harbor, and standing among
The stony cliffs along the shore, all singing in the polyphony

Of Hildegaard von Bingen, and she informs me that
They protect the city, that they turn away the ships of enemies

And guide the vessels of its friends. Then I ask her about
The ranks of men harvesting the ripe coastal grass for haying,

And she answers me that this is one example how husbandry
Is inculcated into the society, that in another life

Many of the men seen harvesting were proponents
Of selfish means, who favored plundering the earth for profit

Instead of managing the balance of her natural ways.
Aboard the cutter in the dream with the wind in our hair,

She speaks a poem about wreathing a rainbow in the sky
On the day before she died, after a night of heavy rain,

In the book that glows with the images of her beloved Vilnius,
After I turn out the light on the night table, her poems page

Through my mind with the icons of their images of wild

Chamomile, plum blossoms, and bitterns contained

In the lyrics. Dandelion honey, the red of the autumn sage,
The mother-of-pearl clouds about to vanish from the sky

Like the great wings of the sea eagle, who is no longer lonely;
And as dusk is extinguished on its wings, her white hair

Changes again into the black hair of her youth, as I awaken
From the dream with the sound of the cutter still in my ears.

Windhorse
Slabs of white marble in stacks.
The pictographs carved in them.

Then this thin tablet. My hands
running across the intaglio of a frieze.

Its smoothness in relief.
The celebration of *Bacchus* in honor

of *Equus*.
Unearthing the actual vision of it

in the archeology of dream.
The going to and the digging through

layers of consciousness, as in layers
of earth.

In the city of *Equestrium.*
That is what I heard. The word spoken

as it was spoken.
Workers and trainers

moving here and there, as in a kind
of bas-relief.

Then someone speaking
to me, instructing me with the urgency

in their stentorian voice.
Although I did not

necessarily know the language.
Then the muscular flanks shining,

a chiseled kind of strength.
The natural aesthetic of the uncut mane.

The sheer beauty of it.
Then putting my foot in the boot

of the narrow stirrup,
I inhaled the fragrance of the leather

before hearing it creak with my weight,
and I settled into the saddle

on the breadth of the massive back.
Before I could even think, the wind

in my hair, the mane flying.
Ride, the voice said, and I did—

in the timeless instant
before awakening from the dream.

Jüri Talvet
Estonia

Building Chairs is Science
> *To the memory of dear Richard Caddel, friend and poet,*
> *with the wish that he could return tomorrow at ten.*

Did the rabbit taste good? Fine.
The salmon? Well. The world's
pulse under your eyelids is indeed
a fine image. (At least you can
feign sleep.) The noble union
of physics with poetry: It's fine
that one can at least relax
into the groove of a bar stool in a
warm small town in Georgia. (If
there's room.) In both Delhis, however,
when it grows dark, only thinking
of gods in a temple, with a cool stone
in the knees, redeems one from the jungle.
Did what's on the grill taste good? I'm glad. I
am happy. How was the chicken? I weave
a spider web for some stranger to get
caught in. Some other from far away,
on the edge. Some Indian cow,
covered with Hegel's grey, boiled
spider web. (Thank you, Heinrich!)
You say you really won't go? You
shall go tomorrow morning at ten.
And you will return tomorrow
morning at ten. Won't you?

*

The swaying train teeters nearer the brink unwillingly
I notice in your voice that you are tense mister JT Is
there no one to stroke your hair? The salvage yard
at the border reads as a permanent installation
of group sex a symbol of the despair of an age
A cloud of seagulls obscures the sky Its explanation
is the neglected skull of a dump between snow fields
Bison never actually grazed in Buffalo though
camels with double humps and double meaning have been
abundant always on both sides of the border Heigh-ho
this high over the canyon one gasps for breath!
The camera caught far below the bristling
of the river's broad back before Niagara breaks it

241

on its knee Tor-onto-onto-onto-onto-onto-onto
the train sings Nobody can pull love's axes from
the heart's knotted stump Between the triple time of
Strauss's joy waltz there is room for the pain of the entire
sea voyage the blood voyage – even though for a while
your fluttering skylark's nest cupped in the palm of my hand
objected each night with courage and frailty

Letter from Venice
From Ljubljana's early Christmas snow
(horse meat was offered there
                              as a national meal,
and Vanesa saw me to the train, undaunted
by shoes thoroughly soaked with sleet)
I found myself under the starry sky of Venice.

For a long time I wandered along the canals.
Not a single Desdemona, though on Rai Uno
I could watch plenty, playing with satyr-stallions.
I thought of Anna,
Italian but from Ljubljana
(she had studied science in Scotland),
Anna, darker than night, who travels from conference
to conference, who sips coffee from a paper cup,
who conjures with powerpoint
images of American e-books.

(Well, Portia too hoodwinked the Jew, to get
her man of the right breed)

So I walked the canals
until I tired, the arrows "San Marco"
and "Piazzale di Roma" vanished into darkness.

Water slept in the canals. My mind was
burdened with beauty, my way lost.
Nor did I know which direction blood took
circulating around my bones,
under my skin, from what shore to what shore.

242

Or maybe the same wave broke
simultaneously on several shores.

Thomas Townsley
United States

The Surrealist's Rose
Borne across serpentine dunes by a caravan of fire ants,
The blood-dripping rose   Bitter vortex

Borne to the edge of a scabrous sea, too salty for dreams,
Rose of holy fire   Map of time's fugue

The sea extends a foaming finger and touches you.
It touches petal and thorn.
At once it ceases mirror-making.
The stars retract their needles of light.
The moon, so lonely it would die for a single petal's caress,
Withdraws its reflection forever.

Hieratic rose   Death's doorbell

Big Tom's All-Nite Diner
Sal's frying orchids in the back,
the hair on his knuckles soon ready for harvest.
The radio is tuned to the amnesia station.
Maggie The Shy Waitress explains to Table Six
that her life is governed by unremembered dreams
—"the invisible armature beneath
all my decision-making," etc. etc.
The man in the eye-patch orders meteor showers.

How long have you been here, alone at the counter?
How long have you been one of the "regulars"?

Now, as you watch, a valent mist the color of wet paper
accumulates outside the window, dissolving the street, erasing every place

from which you might have come, while in their corner booth two young
lovers who "just ducked in to escape the rain"
read their menus silently, without comprehension.

John Trause
United States

Countdown
Because the sun never sets on Oxford University Press,
because grandfathers fart, but not grandmothers,
because the Ashkelon babies were boys, not girls,
because scallions are neither leeks nor chives, nor shallots,
we shall pop the ripe pimple of peace
and count our blessings and bless the count.

Traumnovelle
Hey, Drew, I'm here in Montclair, at Raymond's having dinner with Dr.
Mengele. There seem to be a lotta twins here, so naturally he has a hard-on.
I keep telling myself that this must be a dream, but I don't think so. If you're
free, stop by.

What is Surrealism?
sparked an epidemic of juvenile obesity among the Albanian diaspora
enthusiastic Vortigern with counterpoise as sanctioned by St. Collodion of
Mayagüez Stalin-lipped, heh heh, get it in the house, babydoll.

They were uncertain when Zia Marta mentioned "junk in the trunk". Not
good. I'll crush all your toy(s).

protesting the marwanification of new jersey, teasing treasure chest of dolly
partonismus

deathbed lincoln diagonal   fragonard baise boucher

get me out of here

Bjag Turing
United States

Peacock Angels in God's Tree
God naps like he does every hour and then echoes in a glass
bowl.

There is no light. There is no sea.

Captain Fantastic, you're a piece of meat. You were the captain who
organized the light, and you were poor and solitary. Scribe to a book of
absurd beauty, you sift the soggy black sand and when the light refracts at
night into your eyes, you lash out, and like a hungry eye focus on the hollow
cell. In that moment the toll of light is just a song the sailor sings.

I stare back at the paper sun, its birds glinting in night, the moonjar like
cigarette lids, the stars and planets in the gale.
No wind. With ink of rain and lightning quill he storms the moon, quick as
his dream lover's hips of fire, and drops down
from the scarlet night.

No pain. I am the hand of revelation, and you are the phantom kissing your
way back in southern Spain,

scrawling a green poem in Arabic in the white sun.

Nietzsche
Butterflies danced on the memory of Nietzsche,

who wept for humanity, who wept to tell the history of his tongue; of how he
sounded and the blare of clocks he pronounced with an alphabet of Greek
letters. He griped about the climb up to the light, saw its mirror was waiting, a
mouth of fire with endless mouths to slur. He held his face, "Tell me, how did
you feel, behind the face?"

Some things that looked real to him: a stuffed man with blood across his
chest, a stuffed woman with her breathing cyst, a striptease dancer with her
breasts, a Greek at her back, wet with Old English, a stuffed horse with

245

browned out legs, a stuffed bird with brown fur on its head, a woman with its legs cut off from the human way vomiting ivory stars for his reading list, so that soon he plans his own death.
The full horror of the act.

Thrashing awake, Nietzsche mumbles, What? Whats next? He scrawls. His teeth are bone. The wind teases him like a sickle.

And then he is dead.

Philip Venzke
United States

Odor of Sanctity
There is an obscene elephant
rotting in the living room corner
and we keep bumping into it.
Seems it was a wedding present
that we were afraid to open.
Now it's too late to return it.
We find shells under our pillows
and footprints in our butter.
Our toilet smells of peanuts.
Blind men circle our house.
When epileptic pygmies
are seen arriving after midnight,
we bring in a shaman for aid.
He puts lipstick on clam shells
until coconuts burp from the ceiling
and parrots fart from the walls.
Nothing works. The decay continues.
After the shaman leaves, we amble,
from room to room, turning off lights.
When the night light flickers out,
we hear a snicker.

Dangerous Footprints
The slugs in the garden
decide
with bunions
with corns
with ingrown toenails
to walk
down her cheeks
and the slowness
at which this decision is executed
is so exhausting
that no one notices
the upside down
half buried
derailed locomotive
lying with the tomatoes.

Sarah Webb
United States

Jackrabbit and Coyote Discuss the New Gated Community
We should go down there and check it out, said Jackrabbit.
She watched a concrete mixer back along a drive.
I invited Turtle to come along. Turtle was quite rude about it.
He called me hasty—hasty! He said I rush in and don't think.

Imagine that, said Coyote.

I am not reckless, Jackrabbit snapped. *I just like to get on with*
things.
You'll never find me spun sideways in the middle of the road
like Turtle.

Coyote considered the bulldozers scraping the yucca, didn't say
anything.

Turtle has many good qualities—Jackrabbit gave a thin smile –
but he never made a decision in his life. How he won that wife

247

of his, I cannot fathom.

Slow at love-making, said Coyote, looking at the dust billowing
      from the blades.
Jackrabbit sniffed. *The future's coming at us fast,* she said,
      sharing a thought
that had been on her mind since an encounter with the
      contractor's pickup that morning.
*Look at those house frames. Four houses since yesterday, now
      that's speed.*

They won't be here long, Coyote said.

They won't? Jackrabbit peered at the men unloading pipe.

*Nope. Golf course. And they're putting in sprinkler systems for
      lawns.*

I like lawns, Jackrabbit said.

You would, said Coyote. *Lawns or sagebrush, it's all the same
      to me
as long as there's something to eat when I get hungry.
Speaking of which, it's been a while—*

—since breakfast, he finished. But Jackrabbit was already gone.

Coyote sniffed the dust from the construction site.
No, no chihuahuas yet.

Let There Be Light
In this story,
there was sun from the beginning
always and only
now and ever shall be

but ecstasy too can pall
and grass cannot always be growing.

248

When men stood up and could speak,
more than cattle give tongue or wolves howl,
they complained of thirst
and heat and the blowing dust.
They lay in the shadow of big rocks
and refused to do anything.
Don't want to work up a sweat, they said.

The children cried,
I'm tired, I'm hot, it's glittery!
and their parents said, yeah,
we didn't want to say so, but really!

At last the god thought better of it
and he drew from his shadow
night, said sleep,
said, all right then.

But even then those folks complained.
We're not ready to go to bed,
it's boring, can you tell us a story?
So he gave them dreams.

Dorit Weisman
Israel

Bolivar
1.
I photographed a woman in Bolivar Square.
A Columbian.

I wanted a close-up of her mahogany face
but she moved away, spread her arms obliquely
and flew

and so I photographed her against the background of a gothic
      cathedral

the Andes Mountains and blue sky and white clouds

2.
She was amazed I chose to photograph her,
por que, why

and I replied, bonita,
in other words, you're beautiful

The statue of the revolutionary Bolivar squinted at us from the
            square
the gothic cathedral smiled

Peace talks with leaders of guerilla organizations
continued

Her white teeth gleamed
bonita

Les Wicks
Australia

We Made It, It Made Us
Left the trees
& the junk beast rode us into town.

These houses! Such shelter, rain must hate it here.
We dread the monster but feed its puppies.

Cute as bottletops they snarf down anything that moves.
Amidst stainbows of discarded shopping bags
our life is sealed.

Staunch as dumped fridges, bright as tyrefires
we can depend. Must depend.

A genus of mountaineer, we create our own mountains

with garbage. Last season's *essentials* are flags at the pinnacles.

These peaks will last forever —
our legacy, our proof.

Serrated fingertips wake me up.
Sunday talks but I'm distracted by the blood.

Here in the herd there's so much busyness
who has time to catalogue predation?

Perhaps the Adventure
or maybe just the peacocks, their pecks. Paris, 1940.
Les Boches have lined up our Gauloises & shot them.
Plus, the internet hasn't even been invented.

Klaus thinks Feminism is all about the Jews.
Who said monstrosity can't be flexible —
those Aufseherinnen —
given a real job by clueless men but
Women in Uniforms, they get ideas.

As America undergoes a talking-to
intrepid British spies bugger each other
like tertiary educations.

Kristallnacht is a brand of champagne —
everything makes sense
if you forget energetically.
Pétain has been reading about Panama…
he has niggles over the mosquito problem, the heat
& when accosted by humidity
that way pianos so easily warp into jazz.

Paris must be preserved!
Think of all the movies to come
Hepburn, Marlon, Woody, Kate Hudson.

251

The last lies are progress.
81 years later
the Arc de Triomphe is fake news.
Ex-colonies simmer & refuse
those grand plans imposed on them yet again.
Such ingratitude, like malignant toffee
thank god it sticks in their throats.

Railway Town
Where I grew up there was respect for the uniform.
No one ever killed in them. Armed with timetables
the wise station men & women handled the public
like important post, parcels of love.

On the 2nd floor of the 19th century schoolhouse
serious career advisors charted my promotion…
Station Master if I only *applied myself.*
Snuck off for a smoke out the back
while they enthused lamely to recidivist Timmy
on the life of a shunter.
Were our limitations already infused
into our stubbled DNA?

This is a cogent universe.
In the goods yard,
on an icy nightshift in Outer Junction
my older brother James lost his right arm.
They reassigned him to Correspondence —
one-handed, two-finger typed missives
trickled into the mail chutes for the next 40 years.

Our local university eschewed anything practical
so I graduated with a nuanced world view
alongside no prospects beyond the Transit Recruitment Office
where I professed a love for signal boxes
& got groped by a senile physician — the "physical".

My parents cried at the ceremony
when I was awarded braided epaulettes.

That gold crown badge on my midnight peak cap
shone like a quietly proud moon.
Anywhere in the world
a fellow railworker will give you shelter.
This community of Process,
engraved conclusions,
nothing I've seen elsewhere can compare.

All my life has been ordered.
I knew cars never made sense.
Successive governments & technology
were just rustles in the trees.
Lines became electrified, then duplicated.
The Rail Way is the answer.

My grandchildren are strangers
living far away in computers
but I won the 2014 Station Garden Competition.

Scott Wiggerman
United States

Souvenir of Love
When heartstrings were matchbooks
and a bow moaned loud as a cocktail napkin,
scratched out calligraphic lettering
like huge Art Deco scar tissue.

When your quiet space reversed colors,
and the spotlight of anguish—a forked tongue,
the matches themselves—entered the stream,
a three-inch tall gravity all your own.

When the shocking black hole of grief
ensnared you like a 50¢ luncheon special,
a 75¢ dinner entrée, like red tadpoles
swimming in a double-sized cocktail.

253

A continental color scheme illuminated
five-pointed stars of red, black, and gold,
a crush of circles with a chef's smiling face.
Celestial tipping was never permitted.

Then you accepted a gleaming white toque,
an upscale wild card from your sleeve,
a white-tablecloth restaurant only you
remembered, small as the world's
expensive and expansive lies.

Shit Unhappens
The anus unpuckers. Sphincters wind up. The brain receives and
returns a message from the anus. Food debris and bacteria fill the anus from
the sigmoid colon, where it's been gathering like a landfill. Waste unliquifies
as it tubes through a six-foot runnel of colon, pushing up through the cecum
into the cistern of the small intestine. The liver returns unprocessed nutrients;
the gallbladder leashes bile to dry up and undigest fat; the pancreas excretes
enzymes, building up proteins and carbs that trench up through a sluice to the
duodenum. Muscles in the abdomen swell. A paste called chyme unforms.
Enzymes and acids unmold into larger scraps, channel the mass up into the
holding tank of the stomach. The esophageal sphincter closes, unpressures.
forces the mass up the esophagus. Muscles in the throat suck the bulk higher.
The throat reguritates it. Salivary glands unlubricate the food. Tongue and
teeth recompose it. Teeth ungrind it. Food enters the mouth.
made in China
made in the USA—
same old shit

Furled and Unfurled
After the last bone,
hearts conscripted to stillness,

each wanted brandy, cigarettes.
Flesh fatted on flesh

like cicadas in gun-shot oaks,
hungers bled and harvested.

No more youth, no cues
oncoming, no brass nor tympani,

just low castanets, heavy shadows,
grief tethered to ravens.

After the feast unfurled,
nothing but an abandoned chassis.

Bill Wolak
United States

The Seepage of Dreams
Already naked, she loosens her hair
over skin that's sleek as a sandbar
just returned to the shore by the tide.

Already naked, the sky steps forward
in her eyes with the curiosity of silk,
and wherever you touch her first
feels smoother than bending moonlight.

When she sighs, lightning hesitates.
When she moans, shadows ignite.
When she spreads her legs wider than time,
light is freed from its burden of direction,
and when she trembles, flesh deepens
with the seepage of dreams.

The Keeper of Strangeness
I am the light's fever in honey.
I am the lullaby heard in a nightmare.

In black-eyed alleys
and along tide calloused wharves,
I am the room where you find what you're missing.

I am the dial tone flesh of frightening energy transfers.
I am the expectant hands hovering over nakedness
and the insomnia of sperm.
My lap is a toolshed reaching dreamward.

I am the scarecrow made of birds.
I am the inexhaustible memory of salt.

Out of anger, I created the wind's solitude;
out of love, the restlessness of the rain's long inhalations.

I am the scream's only bridegroom.

SFear of Almanacs
I've opened to the year
of dancing scorpions.
Desire will disappear into museums
where docents will explain
the allure of nakedness.
Phones will stop ringing,
and screens will go blank.
Woodcutters will abandon
their axes in stumps.
This year death and destruction
will linger as close as a pair of aces.
Shifts in the magnetosphere
will cause the seasons to go haywire.
Someone you once loved
will become a yawn of sand
right in front of your face.
You will look out on the sea
and its odor will only remind you
of the unforgettable stench
of the slaughterhouse.
You will become the moth
swimming in candle wax.
Your body will be outlived
by heat lightning.

The undertaker's final offer
will sound like a good deal.
Orpheus will not return
to sing the darkness
out of the underworld.

Elana Wolff
Canada

Forward
The girl with little
fingers pulls big dreams
from her head like
rabbits: albinos on their

hind legs dancing two-step,
tuning kazoos. Out of
jokes, & if any
remain, they're the kind

with little wiggle room
or food they like
to choose from: fresh
vegetables, artisanal bread, vegan

cheese & butter; bottled
water. May all the

little bigsters bow, kowtow
to their freeness, flatten

their squares to four-word
lines: quatrains + a couplet.

The Randomness of Hearsay
According to reports she left her husband
for a shut-in who was found to have a pancreatic

growth. According to the follow-up, she
fled the city after he passed, flew to a place

where no one knew her number.
Madagascar, Montenegro, Gozo, or Djibouti.

The randomness of hearsay is a man in thin pink knits.
Some say

swerve's a synonym for *switch*,
and that may be, but they don't behave

the same way in a poem. Some say poems are
of the soul and must come through the throat.

Metaphysical claims don't get you shelter.

I swear I saw her crossing the freeway naked
the other day ~ hair in the air like helio-red electric ~

Where in hell was she headed? What
was she thinking?   the switch turned off.

Gregory Woods
United Kingdom

The Dog that Flew
He is not one to be petted
Or humbled by tricks with chocolate drops
Nor will being taken for a walk
Satisfy the call of nature, let alone
His lust for adventure. When I first
Saw him, pointed out to me by
A Jehovah's Witness on my own doorstep,

He was alternately pasty on rainclouds
And as black as boots against the

Sulky dusk, swooping down to some Heathrow
Of a recreation ground, with his forepaws
Still retracted and his ears swept back.
'Well, there's something,' said the unwelcome Witness,
Shading her eyes with a free tract.

I went back to my photos of
Lads in various states of undress and
Abandon, meaning to pick out a favourite
To focus on. The one who seemed
Unapproachable on account of his thick hands
and the way his expression dared you
Not to drop to your knees in submission

(For all that he was barely eighteen)
Gave the least reason for being overlooked;
But I could not avoid cocking a
Distracted ear at the window to listen
Out for some kind of canine chirrup.
How could I tell if his silence
Was intended or a sign of vacancy?

I have since got used to the
Sight of him wheeling over a find
Of mass graves or gliding home after
An evening out at the White City.
I think he recognises us who people
His routine; at any rate, I expect
Him to acknowledge me sooner or later.

In a sky as still as cement
His confidence stretches to looping the loop,
But he is never what you could
Call reckless. He keeps his eyes open
And at any given moment can state
Exactly where the day's balloons and kites
Are and what they are up to.

Besides, aerobatics are not quite the point.

Whenever necessary, he can get from A
To B in a fraction of the
Time it would take a champion greyhound;
And research is beginning to suggest that,
Granted a certain amount of private investment,
His skills could have a military application.

Maybe one day the sight of him
Exceeding the strain of his vapour trail
Will be the only friend I need.
A flying dog? I see no reason
Why not. Apart from the question of
Wings and so forth, it makes not
Perfect but only slightly shop-soiled sense.

Jeffrey Cyphers Wright
United States

The Quick Key
Ever-shrinking path to glory's kennel,
sunset's corsage smudges the Hudson.

Cormorants command black pilings.
Loneliness spreads grape kush wings.

Who says you have to work late?
Who insists you flirt with posterity?

Time races on in a black Thunderbird,
ashes knocking at the fire door.

Who says you need to guard the EXIT?
A burning submarine fingering the sea.

Fun melts away as you polish light,
chasing the hounds of fame.

Razor-thin euphoria is a wake-up call.
The party is here—inside these cells.

Hyperion Takes a Hit

Surrounded by invisible naked ladies
I haunted alleyways of wrecked burgundy.
Listening to Heitor Villa-Lobos's fantasies.

What I like is starter fluid on Bozo's grave.

Demand Eternity (but settle for ectasy).
Malappropiation Strategies, for instants:
Custard's Last Stand;
20,000 Leaks Under the Sea.

IOUs dripping from the sun's blind spot.

What kind of fuel am I?

My arms still brag about holding you up
in night's watch-repair shop.

Fire lost in your lips I find abandoned.
There are only green lights in Go Town.

Peter the Great

A few clouds in the south proceed apace.
My days are made of such lost parades.

Helen Hooker plays a madrigal on QXR.
Red coxcombs spurt wrinkled flame.

Homing geese seek the horizon's navel.
Sunset flares, a halo behind your hair.

Life is swell and you are a lucky charmer.
The sugar-frosted Snow Moon beams.

Under your spell, on top of *der Welt*.
Submersed in the champagne of your wake.

Your lips touch mine, softly idling, like
a getaway car. Lightning on your breath.

This is what I live for, to be here, inside
the glow only majesty can bequeath.

Robert Wynne
United States

Salvador Dali's "Girl with a Pearl Earring"
A tower of marble
draped in bronze tapestries
rises to an alabaster neck

that is nothing but bone.
Her red lips are comprised
of peonies in full bloom

and her languid eyes
swivel to look behind you.
Her headscarf is a river

giving itself to gravity,
its long frothy fall
washing a horde of ants

from her shoulders.
The lone silver orb
adorning her left lobe

is a cracked egg from which
something with wings
is about to emerge.

John Yau

United States

After I Turned Sixty-Five

I start asking my co-workers if any of them want to rub my
        invisible tattoos
I tell neighbors to ponder clarity as if it is something that can be
        grasped
I pretend to be an insubordinate squirrel at family gatherings
I memorize how to be vile in different languages
I take up designer drugs and change my taste in music
I secretly keep track of all the people who call me "Pops"
I burn down my childhood tenement in a gentle fashion
I try different styles and flavors and announce that none of them
        suit me
I call a halt to all relationships that smack of the personal
I babble whenever someone asks me for directions
I tell lies about my adolescence in order to impress strangers with
        my pain
I learn to make the sounds of a man who is happily surprised
I insulate myself with voice mail and incompetence

Midway

I did not write a hauntingly beautiful book
No one was haunted by the words I wrote
Neither they nor the book were beautiful

I did not write a book in which the personal
And political converge. I did not become more
Somber and mature as the years sped by

I did not write poems that were desperate
Bewildered or astonished. I did not plumb the depths
In search of a moral encounter with human principles

I did nothing to revive poetic architectures
I did not take pains to ensure my poems performed
Against a backdrop of political, social and ethical values

263

I did not write a book in which themes and images
Resurface, satisfying the reader who, by now, has become
Increasingly anxious and is in need of comfort

I did not write my poems in either a plain or high style
I did not try to motivate the reader to tears or action
My writing is not considered remarkable for its spiritual force

My poems do not travel across a landscape of cultural memory
They do not strike a dynamic balance of honesty,
Emotion, intellectual depth, and otherworldly resonance

They will not startle you out of your daily anesthesia
They do not map the deepest crevices of the interior self
They cast no light on history's margins, overlooked and neglected

Nor is it sacrilegious to comment on my poems
What they lack, their absence of resonant wit,
What they fail to fulfill, worlds they miss out on

On Turning Sixty
Hi, my name is Sir Geoffrey
I am a limpid nerd.
This doesn't mean
I don't possess
many special qualities.
Or that I am not warm
even sensitive
when summoned
to the head of the line
as I just have been.
My skin tingles
when I pass a cage
full of rabbits.
I like chop suey
except when
It is crammed into a can.
I am a robust marshmallow

four days a week,
but I have been known
to ingest long
strings of meat
when they haven't been
individually wrapped
in plastic.
When you cross
the last threshold,
shed your sacred
dog mask, stranger,
and burst into
tears of unrepentant joy.
This is all I will ever ask.

O Pin Yin Sonnet (28)

They cannot say that they invented the atom bomb
They keep crickets in cages and listen to frogs
They don't like to use a knife and fork
They don't drink milk and prefer to eat pigs
They use a different horoscope than one in the Sunday newspaper
They cry when no one is looking and they don't count their tears
They don't write words that can be translated into English
They brush in their suns with dusty black ink
They know how to stop juices from flowing to the brain
They claim to have invented spaghetti but they don't eat waffles
They like to keep their old people alive as long as possible
They venerate the dead as if they were still sitting beside you
They spit on the sidewalk while talking with their friends
Their hair is great for wigs and they are good at manicuring

A View of the Tropics Covered in Ash

I began lying to myself at regular intervals, stopping by the side of the road only when it was necessary. The vegetation did not improve even as the interludes of pleasant shrubbery and herbaceous plants changed, and the waterfalls eventually became walls smothered in stains. I got tired of following myself back to the place where I was delivered; a howling newborn already indoctrinated that the mandibles of doom awaited me, along with other taunts and temptations too

265

monstrous to mention. I did not have to sit long. We must all make dung, announced the boy with a smile full of crooked teeth. This was in the lobby where the first assignments were handed out. Where did you get those pearly gravestones screamed his toothless sister? What do you mean what do you mean moaned another vehicle headed for bedlam in an elastic waistband.

Life in an upscale suburb isn't bad once you get used to hell. The suburban pageantry of soccer played with plastic skulls and rapacious bugs on a green summer day is worthy of an opera, complete with pouting male and curvaceous diva. Drug stores that deliver licensed drugs and pastel condiments are not to be sneezed at. There are plenty of tonics guaranteed to cure baldness, but impotency is something to be proud of, since it means your contributions to civilization's convulsions are dwindling at an accelerated rate.

This is the time to begin concentrating on flying carpets, inexpensive episodes, and sitting in a rowboat on a speckled lake, dreaming of that moment long ago, when the first lie came to you unbidden. You are sleeping under a tree that reaches up past the bottom layer of starlit clouds. The lower branches are burning, just as you planned.

Dean Young
United States

Opaque Presentation
It's weird, since you left
how I'm the one cut out of the photographs.
I look where I used to be and there's a much more
appealing smear. I look where you used to be

and say, There's no point in saying anything, right?
Gnawing on something getting cold, you concur,
growing leathery wings and taking off
without even a single teaspoon of your dog's ash.

After a while, it's easiest to love what doesn't exist
and skip that intermediary discovery part
and eventual tearful groping in the dark phase.

Any diamond is a billion diamonds

once you really look at it, once
you get on your knees and get trapped inside,
everything wobbling at the seams.
Not just anyone can wash their face with an icicle

or brush their teeth with vodka,
you have to have a mind of blackbirds for a long time,
you've got to familiarize yourself with screaming
while not making a sound. Who can believe

what passes for birdsong in these parts anyway?
Everyone deserves their own sky to be hoisted in.
Just because we're only given one life
doesn't mean we don't die countless times.

Progress Report
Escapism was one plan.
Gentrification another.
Some indiscriminate prestidigitation,
lands annexed, slums undone,
abandoned warehouses laced
with coffee shops, rivers redrawn
between the fluctuating forces of oblivion
between people, flotsam and jetsam,
between red argument and white whine,
a few colorful yokels spicing up
the election by championing new drugs,
think keener, dance higher, never cry
but it all comes down to recycling,
schools and rerouting traffic.
Children, should you catch one, often
seem pale and confused like ficus
under tarps, the disquieting results
of misguided primate research funds.
You've got to be careful what studies
you volunteer for. Usually when they show you

pornographic inkblots, they're really interested
in something else. Sewage management for instance.
How far you'd go electrocuting someone else.
You'll be given a blue pill but your symptoms
will be yellow. The one you love lies
about everything. It's all pieces of different
puzzles somehow jangled together.
Is this world just condensing vapor,
dew of evaporating dream?
You'll know when we do.

If Anyone Asks
tell them just because they can't hear the moon
doesn't mean it's not screaming.
Tell them it's just like being attacked
by a murderous lunatic in your own bathroom mirror
or by your own jewelry or toothbrush or taco
or panthers entirely in the mind panthers.
It's like being handed a key
and it drops right through your open palm.
Every 30 seconds another wing goes missing.
Every 10 a breathing machine's turned off.
Anyone who's ever snapped
a rubber band in their own face
or tried to write a poem not dictated
by a bogus institution gets exposed
to some mighty whichway winds.
Everything is made of jumps.
The sentence is always Life,
crepuscular hatchling fallen into the hand
like one of your own organs,
weird stuff coming in the mail,
creepy bouncy rubber eye, Neptunian quartz,
once a broken cobwebby crypt-smelling
music box from the unknown.
Maybe the unknown still loves me.
Maybe it wants me dead.
A horse comes halfway out.

The ballerina has no legs.
Most of what we're made of
comes from outer space
and wants to get back there.
A banana is a berry, a loofa
a gourd, the strongest glue on earth
is made by a whelk. Just try to intervent
the ambulance. Try to get some nerve.
Spiders, scientists assure us, could eat
the entire human race in less then a week
should they ever get in the mood.
Yellow mood of Van Gogh's poison.
Numbered mood of a tax return.
Here, I made a list. A neon larva
twists itself a pupa from a single silken mood.
The soul is fletched. The soul is dashed
across the Hertzsprung-Russell diagram.
Is reality just a failure of the imagination?
That's not what the dandelion thinks
breaking through the asphalt. Not what
the sprinkles on your cupcakes signal.
Sometimes pressure creates electricity
but we always risk dust
in the confetti factory of the ant farm of consciousness.
People always try to turn me off
whenever I mention the Ant Farm of Consciousness
capitalized or not but if my mother
couldn't find an off-switch, good luck.
Ecstasy is willingness.
I dare you to find a river any other way.
I dare you to breathe.
Some cries never reach us
even though they're our own.
The best endings are abrupt.

The Obscurist
You can't grab blossoms.
You can only grab god. You can't

grab god, you can only be dissolved
in the waterfall, spit at by snakes—
a busy morning. I know there's something
I still can't live without but aside from
the mammorial hollers of monkeys
in my dreams, I got neither fin
nor fur to latch onto. Watched a cat
do magnificent battle with the invisible.
Almost touched a human breast. Reached
into the scummy zoo pond water
to retrieve what I swear was a flamingo
feather so shouldn't there be tons of
feathers round here to break my fall?
Shouldn't there be some directions somewhere
probably in Chinese. Which are very helpful.
To the Chinese. Light fuse. Place on ground
and we all know what happens next. Someone
drops the vase, right? The one with calla lilies.
Someone insists the whole mess is mine.
My mother wanted me to be a neurologist
yet it was me she sent under the house
to drag out the dead possum. Death
is a waste of liquidation. I was given
a mechanical rabbit as instruction.
Something inside us is always counting
backwards. We enter through zero.
Even in rapids, may we find rest.

Stunt Man
To have dreamed my love entirely snowflakes.
To have kicked a bookcase in the night.
To wake with spider legs on the pillow case
and for once know where the pain comes from.
To have stepped on a tiny glass hummingbird.
To stare into a corner of the mind
and pull the Hanged Man.
To pinken some sputum.
Oh I don't know how to live without you.

To write something that stupid.
It puts things in perspective, falling down the steps
regardless the condition of the birthday cake.
Yes to the wax chorus melting off its heads.
Yes to tattooed thorns around my wrist
and going back to have the blood-drips touched up.
Yes to a cardiologist who can take a joke.
It's a good day to wear my only good white shirt
like a dare, like an expiration date.
To watch a red dress blow out a window.
A locust evicting its former self.
A tube leaking something blue.
Oh I don't know how to live without you.

Andrena Zawinski
United States

Dancing with Neruda's Bones
Neruda, only known to me in the poet's words—
I love you as certain dark things are to be loved,
in secret, between the shadow and the soul—
Neruda's bones have been exhumed for examination.
I did not want his decomposed body uprooted
from its plot, transmogrified into murder mystery.

Poet of eternal present, I cradle his imagined bones
and pull them to me, his tango body's phalanges
jangling as I cross and giro tibia and fibula—
pinned by the sun between solstice
and equinox, drowsy and tangled together
clanking across tiles of a kitchen floor.

Let Neruda be, I plea, still dancing, his bones tethered
to my body tripping and swaying in tango rhythm,
talking head on the radio droning on
in conspiracy theories of the Pinochet regime
poisoning Neruda, life split in poetry and politics

271

as *the night wind whirls in the sky and sings.*

Forecast of ill fortune—to lift bones from the grave—
much like this wave of melancholia. In inevitable
surrender, I concede: what does it matter
to have dug them up as his love lyrics resonate
in his monotoned moan, Gardel crooning
behind our bumpy boleo: *el dia que me quieras.*

Neruda's unearthed skeleton clings to my arms,
scent of honeysuckle climbing limbs like vines,
as I sweep and dip inside his metaphoric sigh of sea
and our final soltada—*voice of the rain crying:*
no carnations or barcaroles for me,
only a wound that love had opened.

Neruda, now so mystical and magical,
cloaks his bones in flesh and play, conjures
a dusty fiddle, leaps and lands on the walkway below,
the violin with its ragged companion...
learning how to befriend lost souls
and sing songs to wandering strangers.

Jonas Zdanys
United States

from Notebook Sketches
I was lifted up by a great black bird,
beyond the tracks, beyond the fall
of water, in a dark alley shrouded in fog
when the flame sawed and the day
lashed and the ghosts on the rooftops
stirred. All of them are gone except
for me, the iron ascending when black
birds flicker in the scales of their long
descent. It was where the street turned

272

left off the main road, near the edge
of town where the roofs were flat
and the windows long and the houses
narrow and bare. The floor creaked when
I went outside to listen to the voices
that gathered in that other night,
my cold hand inching across the barren
circle, the dust on the stairs pushing
words into my mouth in response.
There was something past the statue
in the square, a shadow floating
in the moonlight, the night holding
its breath, that led me to an empty
space pinned against the light.
A single word floated up from the past.
An unpredictable scrawl numbed the moon.
I stood to let the darkness rise.
And I was falling, falling, like a meager wall,
falling bleak when the street rebelled, and
when I turned, transfixed, dark wings took hold.

*

The light in the kitchen of the house
next door goes out. They are suddenly
blind, trembling to undress, caught
in the sounds of things before the storm.
They stumble in the dark in small circles
hoping to find each other again,
one foot –her right, his left – nailed
loosely to the wide planks of the wooden
floor, each arm waving the thick darkness
of winter away. It was a moment neither
wished to keep, the measure of all things,
of anguish, of lack, knocking on the window,
falling to gray dust that coats the walls.
The moon is obscured but I can see
the shadows of their odd dance.
I am looking for a way out for them,
my hand half-raised, time standing

still, my heart beating. She flaps her
arms like a painted bird in response,
fluttering toward the ceiling, pulled back
by the nail in the floor. He strikes a match.
There is a sudden rush of air.

from Three White Horses

I did not expect to see him through
the interruptions of the gray window:
the odd little man dressed in green
and black turning around in the street
at every third step to count the footprints
he had left behind in the snow, up again
to the yellow stairs that lead to his door:
one foot the frame of a well-worn boot,
the other the foot of a hobbled bird.
He stops and starts like a cold ember, knows
that the clawed foot drags the plow of time,
scratching the earth as it scuttles the west
and paling in the migrant orbits of stars.
He knows that if the burning eye that hangs
above him in the square falls across the sky,
shadows will hollow the walls he stumbles
against, elide the red ash on the doorsills
he hops across on one leg unaware.
He knows the vellum and the flicker,
the involuntary rule that flutters in the charge,
and the woman he has not yet named who
sleeps undone in the bottle and the sash.
His shadow is itself a shadow of a shadow.
His nervous hand still prods the air.
His feet again are cold.
I turn off the lantern in the window
he so watches, lid the burning eye.

Contributors and Permissions Acknowledgments

All of the poems in this anthology are reprinted by permission of their respective authors.

Will Alexander is a finalist for the 2022 Pulitzer Prize in Poetry. He is the author of more than thirty books. *Singing In Magnetic Hoofbeat: Essays, Prose, Texts, Interviews, and a Lecture* (2013) was awarded an American Book Award. His other honors include a Whiting Fellowship for Poetry, a California Arts Council Fellowship, and the 2016 Jackson Poetry Prize. "The Pointless Nether Plow" is from *Compression & Purity*; "Inside the Ghost Volcano," "Above the Human Nerve Domain," and "The Impalpable Brush Fire Singer," are from *Above the Human Nerve Domain*. All are copyright © by Will Alexander.

Greta Ambrazaite is a Lithuanian poet, translator and book editor. Her first book was awarded the Young Yotvingian Prize as best young poet's book in 2018 and Poetry Book of the Year 2018 in Lithuania. In 2019 she was awarded the Young Artist's Prize by the Lithuanian Ministry of Culture. Poems copyright © by Greta Ambrazaite and Rimas Uzgiris.

Iván Argüelles, a Mexican-American poet, is the author of many books. A retired librarian, he was employed by the New York Public Library and The Library of the University of California at Berkeley. His collection *Looking for Mary Lou* received the 1989 William Carlos Williams Award from the Poetry Society of America. Poems copyright © by Iván Argüelles.

Cassandra Atherton has published thirty critical and creative books and has received many national and international grants. She is a commissioning editor of *Westerly* magazine, series editor for *Spineless Wonders Microlit* anthologies, and associate editor at MadHat Press. She co-authored *Prose Poetry: An Introduction* (Princeton University Press, 2020) and co-edited the *Anthology of Australian Prose Poetry* (Melbourne University Press, 2020). She is Professor of Writing and Literature at Deakin University, Australia. "Carrying a Watermelon" was published in translation in the Japanese poetry journal, *Gendai-Shi-Techo*); "Fowl" was published in *Leftovers*; "Gingerbread Man was published in *Pleasant Troubles*; "Bonds" was published in *Exhumed*. Poems copyright © by Cassandra Atherton.

Adjei Agyei Baah is co-founder of Africa Haiku Network, Poetry Foundation, and *The Mamba*, Africa's first international haiku journal."The Call" is copyright © by Adjei Agyei Baah.

Jim Barnes, a former Oklahoma Poet Laureate, is the recipient of an American Book Award for his *On Native Ground: Memoirs and Impressions*, and was twice awarded a Rockefeller Foundation Bellagio Fellowship. "Surrealist Poet" is from *Paris*;

Tony Barnstone is the author of twenty books and a music CD. His awards include The Poets Prize, the Strokestown International Prize, the Pushcart Prize in Poetry, The John Ciardi Prize, The Benjamin Saltman Award, and fellowships from the NEA, NEH, and California Arts Council. He has also co-edited several anthologies. "Nightmare Kiss" is from *Sad Jazz: Sonnets*; "Beast in the Apartment" is from *Beast in the Apartment*. Poems copyright © by Tony Barnstone.

Margo Berdeshevsky's latest poetry collection, *Before The Drought*, was a finalist for the National Poetry Series. Her book of illustrated stories, *Beautiful Soon Enough*, received the first Ronald Sukenick Innovative Fiction Award from Fiction Collective Two. Other honors include the Robert H. Winner Award from the Poetry Society of America. "Even With No Hand To Hold It" is copyright © by Margo Berdeshevsky.

Charles Bernstein is the recipient of the 2019 Bollingen Prize for American Poetry. The poems in this volume are used with the permission of the author. "Beyond the Valley of the Sophists," from *Rough Trades* (Sun & Moon Press, 1991); "Chimera," from *Recalculating* (University of Chicago Press, 2013); "Mystic Brokerage," from *Near/Miss* (University of Chicago Press, 2018); an alternate version of "H Marked the Spot (Take Two)," was collected in *Topsy-Turvy* (University of Chicago Press, 2021); "Twelve-year Universal Horoscope," from *Topsy-Turvy* (University of Chicago Press, 2021). Poems copyright © by Charles Bernstein.

Charles Borkhuis has published nine collections of poems and was awarded the James Tate International Poetry Prize for 2021. His *Alpha Ruins* was selected as a finalist for the W.C. Williams Award in 2000. He curated poetry readings for the Segue Foundation in NYC for 15 years and his plays have been presented throughout the United States and in Paris. He is the recipient of a Dramalogue Award and is the former editor of THEATER: EX magazine. Poems copyright © by Charles Borkhuis.

Peter Boyle has nine books of poetry published and eight books as a translator of poetry from Spanish and French. He has received the New South Wales Premier's Award for Poetry in 1995, 2017, and 2020; The Philip Hodgins Memorial Prize for a consistently outstanding Australian writer (2017); NSW Premier's Award for Literary Translation (2013); the Queensland Premier's Award for Poetry and the ARTS ACT Judith Wright Award, (2010); the National Book Council Award (1997); Adelaide Festival Award for Poetry (1998); and the National Book Council Award (1994). "The Joys of Mathematics" is from *Coming Home from the World* and "Missing Words" is from *What the Painter Saw in our Faces*. Poems copyright © by Peter Boyle.

Jerry Bradley is University Professor of English and the Leland Best Distinguished Faculty Fellow at Lamar University. He won the 2017 Boswell Poetry Prize and in 2018 received writing awards from the Conference of College Teachers of English and the Texas College English Association. He is the author of nine books, including six full-length collections. He is the long-time poetry editor of *Concho River Review*, a past-president of the Texas Association of Creative Writing Teachers, the Conference of College Teachers of English, and the Southwest Popular and American Culture Association, which endows a writing award in his name. "The Island of the Dolls" appeared in *South of the Boredom*; "Beauty and the Beast" appeared in *Rapunzel's Daughter*; "Belling the Vampire" appeared in Crownfeathers and Effigies; "Mischance" appeared in *Simple Versions of Disaster*; "A Field Guide to Dreams" appeared in *The Importance of Elsewhere*. Poems copyright © by Jerry Bradley.

John Bradley's *Spontaneous Mummification* won the James Tate Poetry Prize. He is recipient of two National Endowment for the Arts Fellowships and a Pushcart Prize. He serves as assistant editor for *Cider Press Review* and reviews books for *Rain Taxi*. "Placental Gravity" and "Before My First, After My Last, I Wear Dirt's Shirt," were published in *SurVision*; "For Joyce Mansour, Lost in Cairo" was published in *The Room*; "Roundlet: From the Book of Arrested Propulsion" was published in the *Nonmaterialism Foundation*. Poems copyright © by John Bradley.

Zoe Brooks has a blog, magic-realism-books.blogspot.com, and runs the Magic Realism Books Facebook Group. Her long poem Fool's Paradise won the EPIC award for best poetry ebook 2013. She is the author of two books. "There's Nothing to See" and "Dorothy Wilson Said" appeared in *Owl Unbound* and are copyright © by Zoe Brooks.

Sue Burge has work featured in themed anthologies with poems on science fiction, modern Gothic, illness, Britishness, endangered birds, WWI, and the current pandemic. She has four poetry collections. "It Only Happens In My Dreams" was published in *SurVision* and is copyright © by Sue Burge.

Rachel Burns was shortlisted in the Wolves Lit Fest Poetry Competition 2021 and won second place in The Julian Lennon Prize 2021. "Behind the Scenes at the Museum" was published in *SurVision* and "Black Butterflies in *inDivisible*, both copyright © by Rachel Burns.

Casey Bush is an anarchist, in the Spencerian sense, and an underwriter, after the example of Kafka. He picks mushrooms and throws the yo-yo; prefers the golden trumpet over liberty caps and skinning the cat over walking the dog. He lives in Portland, Oregon, which has survived, a little worse for wear, after four years as the training ground for Trump's brown shirted Proud Boys. Poems copyright © by Casey Bush.

277

Garrett Caples has been Editor, City Lights Spotlight Poetry Series, since 2009. Other editorial projects include books by Lamantia, Frank Lima, Stephen Jonas, Richard O. Moore, Samuel Greenberg, and Michael McClure. "Targets and Flowers" appeared in *The Garrett Caples Reader*; "Untitled" and "i have seen enough" appeared in *Complications*; "Love Is Made of Sky" and "Paul Bowles in El Cerrito" appeared in *Power Ballads*. Poems copyright © by Garrett Caples.

Srinjay Chakravarti's first book of poems, *Occam's Razor*, received the Salt Literary Award from John Kinsella in 1995. He has won first prize in the Dorothy Sargent Rosenberg Memorial Poetry Competition 2007-08. "At the Sleepwalkers' Hotel" was published in *Near East Review* and is copyright © by Srinjay Chakravarti.

Lidia Chiarelli is one of the Charter Members of Immagine & Poesia, the art literary movement founded in Torino in 2007 with Aeronwy Thomas, Dylan Thomas' daughter. She was awarded a Certificate of Appreciation from The First International Poetry Festival of Swansea (U.K.) and a Literary Medal from Cross-Cultural Communications; the Sahitto International Prize as winner of the Grand Jury Award 2021; and the Jury Prize Premio Lord Byron, Porto Venere - Golfo dei Poeti 2021. "Land of Magic" was published in *The Seventh Quarry* and is copyright © by Lidia Chiarelli.

Graham Clifford has published five books. All the poems reprinted here are from *In Charge of the Gun* and are copyright © by Graham Clifford.

Brian Clifton is the author of two books and have work in several journals. They are an avid record collector and curator of curiosities. "Scarlet Heaven" was published in *Golden Walkman* and is copyright © by Brian Clifton.

Andrei Codrescu is a Romanian-born American poet, novelist, essayist, screenwriter, and commentator for National Public Radio. He is the winner of the Peabody Award for his film *Road Scholar* and the Ovid Prize for poetry. He was Mac Curdy Distinguished Professor of English at Louisiana State University from 1984 until his retirement in 2009. He was editor and founder of *Exquisite Corpse: a Journal of Books and Ideas* and has published some sixty collections of poetry and translations. Poems copyright © by Andrei Codrescu.

Diana L. Conces has published a novel, a poetry chapbook, and a short story collection. "Avatar" was published in the *Tipton Poetry Journal* and is copyright © by Diana Conces.

Alfred Corn is the author of eleven books of poems, two novels, and three collections of critical essays. He has received a Guggenheim, an NEA award, an Award in Literature from the Academy of Arts and Letters, and an award from the Academy of American Poets. He has been named a Life Fellow at Clare Hall, Cambridge. In

November 2017 he was inducted into the Georgia Writers' Hall of Fame. His translation of Rilke's *Duino Elegies* appeared in 2021. "Brush with Greatness" was published in *X-Peri*; "Alice's Rules" was published in *Jacket*; "At Some Length" and "Cheiromancy" were published in *The Wolf*; "Mickle Street" was published in Poetry. Poems copyright © by Alfred Corn.

MTC Cronin has published over twenty books, including collections jointly written with Australian poet/translator Peter Boyle and Melbourne-based poet/librettist Maria Zajkowski. The poems presented here were published in *Trees Like Grasses ~ sixty micro-prose pairs* and are copyright © by MTC Cronin.

Craig Czury is the author of over twenty poetry collections, several of which have been translated into Italian, Portuguese, Spanish, Croatian, Albanian, and Russian. He is a 2020-22 recipient of a Fulbright Scholarship to Chile.. Poems copyright © by Craig Czury.

Antonio D'Alfonso has published more than fifty books and has made five feature films. He is the founder of *Guernica Editions*. For his writings, he won the Trillium Award and the Bressani Award, and his film *Bruco* won the New York Independent Film Award. His new film, *TATA* (Daddy), was released in July 2020. *The Two-Headed Man: Collected Poems 1970-2020* was published in July 2020. He has started, on youtube, a series of "Conversations" with artists and producers. Poems copyright © by Antonio D'Alfonso.

Subhrasankar Das is from Tripura, India. He is a bilingual poet, a translator, editor, and composer. Poems copyright © by Subhrasankar Das.

Lawdenmarc Decamora is a Best of the Net and Pushcart Prize-nominated writer with work published in twenty-three countries. He was longlisted for the Alpine Fellowship Writing Prize 2021 (UK). He is a college professor. "Self-Portrait as Open Flesh of an Undetermined Panic" was published in *Ilanot Review* and is copyright © by Lawdenmarc Decamora.

Thad DeVassie is a multi-genre writer and painter who lives in Ohio. He was awarded the 2020 James Tate International Poetry Prize. "Ghost Bus" and "Everything is Random" were published in *Splendid Irrationalities*; "Cricket Hymn for the Apocalypse" was published in *This Side of Utopia*, all copyright © by Thad DeVassie.

John Digby was born in London in 1938, and for the last 38 years has lived in Oyster Bay, New York. He began writing Surrealist poetry in the early 1970s, with his first publication of Surrealist poetry in America during the time he worked with George Hitchcock on *Kayak Magazine*. His poetry is included in *The Penguin Book of English Surrealism*. In England, he was the co-founder of Caligula Books. Poems copyright © by John Digby.

Mark DuCharme is the author of many collections. He is recipient of the Neodata Endowment in Literature and the Gertrude Stein Award in Innovative American Poetry. "They Dream" was published in *Colorado Review* and "Stammer" was published in *Caliban Online* no. 32. Poems copyright © Mark DuCharme.

Alison Dunhill had two pieces longlisted for the Fish Flash Fiction Prize in March 2020 and won Second Prize in the 2020 James Tate International Poetry Prize. An art historian, she considers links between interwar surrealism and 1970s US photography.. "Fragments" was published in *Joe Soap's Canoe #15*, then titled "On the Backs of Sheep in Evening Sun." "You Make Me Feel Brand New" was published in *As Pure as Coal Dust*. Poems copyright © by Alison Dunhill.

Alan Elyshevitz is the author of a collection of stories, a full-length collection of poems, and four poetry chapbooks. Winner of the James Hearst Poetry Prize from *North American Review,* he is a two-time recipient of a fellowship in fiction writing from the Pennsylvania Council on the Arts. "Insomnia, Part IX" was published in *Caesura* and is copyright © by Alan Elyshevitz.

John Ennis published his *Later Selected Poems 2000-2020 Going Home to Wyoming* in 2020. His haiku appears in *Trio of Shadows* with Maki Starfield and Kika Hotta. His archive to 2017 is at Princeton. He is working on *Speaking of the Doves*. Poems copyright © John Ennis.

Elaine Equi's latest book is *The Intangibles* from Coffee House Press, and she is the author of fifteen collections. Her work has been widely published and anthologized. She teaches at New York University and in the MFA Program in Creative Writing at The New School. "Gradually, Gills" is used by permission from *Ripple Effect: New & Selected Poems* (Coffee House Press, 2007). All three poems included here are copyright © by Elaine Equi

R.G. Evans is the author of three poetry collections and a horror novella. His collection of original songs, *Sweet Old Life*, is available on most streaming platforms. "All Newborn Gods" and "Yellow Poem, Blue Poem, Red Poem" were published in *Imagine Sisyphus Happy* and are copyright © by R.G. Evans.

Zoë Fay-Stindt (she/they/Z) is a queer, pangender, bicontinental poet with roots in both the French and American south. Z's work has been nominated for the Pushcart Prize. "Her Beak Inside Me" appeared in *fields magazine* and is copyright © by Zoë Fay-Stindt.
Scott Ferry helps our Veterans heal as an RN in the Seattle area. He has three books of poetry. Poems copyright © by Scott Ferry.

S.C. Flynn was born in Australia of Irish origin and now lives in Dublin. His poetry has recently been published in *Abridged, The Waxed Lemon, Beir Bua, SurVision,* and

A New Ulster. Poems copyright © by S.C. Flynn.

Jack Foley has published seventeen books of poetry, five books of criticism, a book of stories, and *Visions and Affiliations*, a history of California poetry 1940-2005. He is currently one of the hosts of Berkeley radio station KPFA's literary program "Cover to Cover." He has received two Lifetime Achievement Awards, one from Marquis *Who's Who* and one from the Berkeley Poetry Festival, and June 5, 2010 was declared "Jack Foley Day" in Berkeley. His most recent books are the companion volumes, *The Light of Evening*, a brief autobiography, and *A Backward Glance O'er Travel'd Roads*, an autobiography of the poet's mind. Poems copyright © by Jack Foley.

Linda Nemec Foster is the author of twelve collections of poetry and has been a finalist for the Ohio Book Award in Poetry, for *ForeWord Magazine's* Book of the Year, and received the 2019 Michigan Notable Book award. Her first commissioned libretto had its world premiere in 2022. From 2003-05, she served as the first Poet Laureate of Grand Rapids, Michigan. In the fall of 2019, she was the poet-in-residence at the University of Bielsko-Biala in Poland. She is the founder of the Contemporary Writers Series at Aquinas College. Poems copyright © by Linda Nemec Foster.

Dede Fox is Poet Laureate of Montgomery County, Texas, and was the 2016-2019 NEA Artist in Residence at Bryan Federal Prison Camp for Women. She currently teaches with WITS-Houston at Texas Children's Hospital. She is the author of four books and has written nonfiction for *Highlights Magazine*. Poem copyright © by Dede Fox.

Jeff Friedman is the author of eight books. He has received a National Endowment Literature Translation Fellowship in 2016 and two individual Artist Grants from New Hampshire Arts Council. Two of his micro stories were recently selected for the *The Best Microfiction 2021.* "Catching the Monster" was published in *Survision* and "Bear Fight" appeared in his *Floating Tales*. Poems copyright © by Jeff Friedman.

Joanna Fuhrman is the author of six books of poetry. She teaches creative writing and organizes the faculty and alumni reading at Rutgers University in New Brunswick. Her essays on teaching poetry appear regularly in *Teachers & Writers Magazine*. The poems here have appeared previously in *Posit, New American Writing, Boog City,* and *The Brooklyn Rail,* and are copyright © by Joanna Fuhrman.

C. M. Gigliotti lives in Berlin. *Blue Muse* magazine awarded her the 2018 Leslie Leeds Poetry Prize. She serves as Poetry Editor of the *Connecticut Literary Festival Anthology*, vol. 2."Rigor (Amor)tis" was published in *The Dillydoun Review*. Poems copyright © by C. M. Gigliotti.

Daniela Gioseffi is an American Book Award winning author of eighteen books of poetry and prose and edits *Eco-Poetry.org*. She has been awarded a New York State Council for the Arts Grant Award, The John Ciardi Award for Lifetime Achievement in Poetry, the OSIA NY State Literary Award, and an American Italian Educators Lifetime Achievement Award. Her women's studies classic *Women on War: International Writings* has been in print for over twenty-five years. She published *On Prejudice: A Global Perspective* (1993) and won a World Peace Prize from The Ploughshares Fund, presented at the U.N. Her work was etched in marble near that of Walt Whitman's and William Carlos Williams's on a wall of Penn Station in New York City. Poem copyright © by Daniela Gioseffi.

Chrissie Gittins writes poetry for adults, poetry for children, short stories, and radio drama. She has published three adult poetry collections and appeared on BBC Countryfile with her fifth children's collection. She has received Arts Council and Author's Foundation awards, she features on the Poetry Archive, and she is a Hawthornden Fellow. "Velcro" was published in *Anthropocene* and is copyright © by Chrissie Gittins.

Ray Gonzalez is the author of fourteen books. He received a 2018 Witter Bynner Foundation Fellowship in Poetry from the Library of Congress. He teaches creative writing in the MFA Program at the University of Minnesota in Minneapolis. Poems copyright © by Ray Gonzalez.

Patricia Goodrich is a poet and visual artist and author of a dozen collections of poetry. She has been featured reader at many international festivals, and is the recipient of Pennsylvania Fellowships in Poetry and Creative Nonfiction. Her poetry has been translated into Chinese, Finnish, French, Lithuanian, Slovenian, and Romanian. "After Picasso" was published in her *How The Moose Got To Be* and is copyright © by Patricia Goodrich.

Ken Hada is the author of nine poetry collections. His work has been awarded by SCMLA, The National Western Heritage Museum, and Western Writers of America, and has been featured on The Writer's Almanac. He directs the annual Scissortail Creative Writing Festival at East Central University in Ada, Oklahoma. Poems copyright © by Ken Hada.

Philip Hammial, originally from Detroit, has been living since 1972 in Australia, where he has had thirty-four poetry collections published. His poems have appeared in more than thirty anthologies in seven countries, and he has represented Australia at fourteen international poetry festivals. Poems copyright © by Philip Hammial.

Oz Hardwick has published nine full collections and chapbooks and has won the 2019 Rubery International Book Award for poetry. He has held residencies in the UK,

Europe, the US, and Australia, and has performed internationally at major festivals and intimate soirees. He is Professor of English at Leeds Trinity University, where he leads the postgraduate Creative Writing programmes. "… to Station" was published in *Learning to Have Lost* and "Bee "was published in *An Eschatological Bestiary*. Poems copyright © by Oz Hardwick.

Nicholas Alexander Hayes is the author of two collections and has published academic essays on 1960s Gay pulp fiction, the television show *Glee*, depictions of masculinity on social media, and the pedagogy of Queer literature. Poems copyright © by Nicholas Alexander Hayes.

Dominique Hecq grew up in the French-speaking part of Belgium and now lives in Melbourne. Her works include a novel, three collections of short stories, eleven books and chapbooks of poetry, and two one-act plays. She has been awarded The Melbourne Fringe Festival Award for Outstanding Writing and Spoken Word Performance, The *New England Review* Prize for Poetry, The Martha Richardson Medal for Poetry, and the inaugural AALITRA Prize for Literary Translation in poetry from Spanish into English. She received the 2018 International Best Poets Prize administered by the International Poetry Translation and Research Centre. "Unfinished Genesis" was published in the *Aesthetica Creative Writing Annual Anthology*, and is copyright © by Dominique Hecq.

Bob Heman is the author of five volumes of poetry. His art includes collages, drawings, and participatory cut-out multiples on paper. His drawings are included in *The Lamp's Tales*, a collection of prose poems by Belgian Surrealist Paul Colinet, and his own prose poems are included in many anthologies and magazines. The poems here are from his *The House of Grand Farewells* and are copyright © by Bob Heman.

William Heyen has earned recognition from the National Endowment for the Arts, the Guggenheim Foundation, the American Academy and Institute of Arts and Letters, the

Fulbright Foundation, and many others, and was a finalist for the National Book Award for his *Shoah Train*. He is the author of many volumes of poetry, short stories, essays, and fiction. "The Tooth" appears in *Crazy Horse & the Custers: The River of Electricity*. Both poems included here are copyright © by William Heyen.

Jack Hirschman, who died as this book was going to press, was an American poet and social activist who wrote more than 100 volumes of poetry and essays. His life's masterwork is "The Arcanes," of which the included poem is an excerpt. It is copyright © by Jack Hirschman.

Heikki Huotari, in another century, attended a one-room school and spent summers on a forest-fire lookout tower. He is a retired math professor. His fourth collection, *Deja Vu Goes Both Ways*, won the Star 82 Press Book Award. The poems here were first published in *When Correlation is Causation* (Better than Starbucks 2021) and are copyright © by Heikki Huotari.

Cindy Huyser's poems have received multiple Pushcart Prize nominations. She was co-winner of the 2014 Blue Horse Press Poetry Chapbook Contest and has edited or co-edited a number of anthologies, including several editions of the *Texas Poetry Calendar*. She has been featured reader in the Houston Poetry Fest, in Houston's Public Poetry series, and the Scissortail Creative Writing Festival. Poem copyright © by Cindy Huyser.

Helen Ivory is a poet and visual artist who has published ten collections. She edits the webzine *Ink Sweat and Tears* and teaches creative writing online for the University of East Anglia/National Centre for Writing. She has work translated into Polish, Ukrainian and Spanish as part of the Versopolis project. The poems here are from her book *Waiting for Bluebeard* (Bloodaxe 2013) and are copyright © by Helen Ivory.

Gerald Jatzek is a poet and musician from Vienna, Austria, who writes in German and English. He has published books for children and adults, short stories, plays for radio, and essays. He received the Austrian State Prize for Children's Poetry in 2001. Poem copyright © by Gerald Jatzek.

Michael Jennings is the author of more than a dozen collections of poetry, for which he has been awarded the Central New York Book Award for Poetry, the Wells College Chapbook Contest prize, and the Miller Audio Award for Poetry offered by *The Missouri Review.* Poems copyright © by Michael Jennings.

Andrew Joron is the author of five collections of poems, a selection of prose poems and critical essays, and translations from the German of the *Literary Essays* of Marxist-Utopian philosopher Ernst Bloch and *The Perpetual Motion Machine* by the proto-Dada fantasist Paul Scheerbart. He teaches creative writing at San Francisco State University. Poems copyright © by Andrew Joron.

Tim Kahl is the author of four collections and editor of *Clade Song*. He is events coordinator of The Sacramento Poetry Alliance and teaches at California State University, Sacramento, where he sings lieder while walking on campus between classes. Poems copyright © by Tim Kahl.

George Kalamaras, former Poet Laureate of Indiana (2014-2016), has published thirteen full-length collections of poems and eight poetry chapbooks. He has received the Elixir Press Poetry Prize and has won the C&R Press Open Competition and the

Four Way Books Intro Series. He also has received an Indo-U.S. Advanced Research Fellowship to conduct research in India, an NEA Fellowship in Poetry, and has twice received an Individual Artist Fellowship from the Indiana Arts Commission. He is Professor of English at Purdue University Fort Wayne. "Inscribed Into Him, Into His Him of Her" first appeared in *Carolina Quarterly*, Vol. 63, No. 3. *"Kingdom of Throat-Stuck Luck" first appeared in the Denver* Quarterly, Vol. 44, No. 1 and was reprinted in the author's book, *Kingdom of Throat-Stuck Luck*. Poems copyright © by George Kalamaras.

Eliot Katz is the author of seven books of poetry and two prose e-books. He was coeditor, with Allen Ginsberg, of *Poems for the Nation*; and served as co-editor of *Long Shot* literary journal, as co-editor of a bilingual anthology titled *Changing America: Contemporary U.S. Poems of Protest*, and as poetry editor of *Logos: A Journal of Modern Society and Culture*. He continues to work as an activist for a wide range of peace, social justice, and human rights causes. Poem copyright © by Eliot Katz.

Anna Keiko is a Chinese poet and writer, president and editor-in-chief of Shanghai Huifeng literature society, director of Ithaca International Foundation, and president of international poetry Promotion Association. She has published three books of poetry and co-authored more than forty other books. Her poems have been translated into more than thirty languages and have won many international awards. Poem copyright © by Anna Keiko.

S. K. Kelen won the 1973 Poetry Australia Award for Australian Poets under 18. His work since then has appeared in journals, ezines, newspapers, anthologies, and broadcast on radio. He is the author of sixteen collections. Poems copyright © by S.K. Kelen.

Charles Kell is the author of *Cage of Lit Glass*, chosen by Kimiko Hahn for the 2018 Autumn House Press Poetry Prize, and *Pierre Mask*, winner of the 2019 James Tate Chapbook Prize. He is assistant professor at the Community College of Rhode Island and editor of the *Ocean State Review*. Poems copyright © by Charles Kell.

Adele Kenny is author of twenty-five books. She serves as poetry editor of *Tiferet* and is the Carriage House Poetry Series' founding director. She is the 2021 first place Allen Ginsberg Poetry Award winner, and has also received New Jersey State Arts Council poetry fellowships and Kean University's Distinguished Alumni Award. One of her books was a Paterson Poetry Prize finalist. "Elegy for the Man Who Collected Keys" was published in *SurVision*. "So Much Life" was published in her book *A Lightness, A Thirst, or Nothing At All*. Poems copyright © by Adele Kenny.

Kerry Shawn Keys is the author of many dozens of books. He received the Robert H. Winner Memorial Award from the Poetry Society of America and a National Endowment for the Arts Literature Fellowship. He was a Senior Fulbright Research grantee for African-Brazilian studies in Salvador, Brazil, and from 1998 to 2000 taught translation theory and creative composition as a Fulbright Associate Professor at Vilnius University in Lithuania. Poems copyright © by Kerry Shawn Keys.

Tony Kitt lives in Dublin, Ireland. His family hails from County Mayo in the West of Ireland, as well as from Tuscany, Greece, and Poland. He has a background in biology, Celtic studies, and classical music, and has worked as a researcher, a journalist, and a creative writing tutor. His poetry chapbook entitled The Magic Phlute has been published by SurVision Books (Dublin, Ireland) in 2019. His collection entitled Endurable Infinity is forthcoming from Pittsburgh University Press in the Pitt Series. His other collection, Sky Sailing, is due from Salmon Poetry in Ireland. His poems also appear in such magazines as Oxford Poetry, The North, Plume, Poetry Ireland Review, The Prague Revue, Cyphers, Under the Radar, The American Journal of Poetry, Stride, etc., as well as in a number of anthologies. In 2022, he edited the anthology entitled Invasion: Ukrainian Poems about the War for SurVision Books. He performed at many festivals across Europe, and in 2003 won the Maria Edgeworth Poetry Prize.

Noelle Kocot is the author of several books of poetry and a volume of translations of poems by the French poet Tristan Corbiere. She is the recipient of numerous awards, including those from The Academy of American Poets, The National Endowment for the Arts, *The American Poetry Review*, and The Fund for Poetry. She teaches writing in New York. Poems copyright © by Noelle Kocot.

Laurie Kolp's poems have appeared in many journals and she is the author of several full-length books and chapbooks. Poem copyright © by Laurie Kolp.

Michael Leong is the author of four poetry books. His co-translation, with Ignacio Infante, of Vicente Huidobro's long poem *Sky-Quake: Tremor of Heaven* was published in 2020. He has received grants from the Council of Literary Magazines and Presses and the National Endowment for the Arts. He teaches at California Institute of the Arts. "from 'Disorientations'" was published in *Hambone 22* and "My teacher said" was published in *Big Other* (September 2019). Poems copyright © by Michael Leong.

Susan Lewis is Editor-in-chief of *Posit* (www.positjournal.com) and is winner of the Washington Prize and the Cervena Barva Press Chapbook Prize. She is author of five collections and several chapbooks. "One Day" was published in her *Heisenberg's Salon* and "All Signs" was published in her *Zoom*. Poems copyright © by Susan Lewis.

Anna Maria Mickiewicz is a Polish-born poet, writer, editor, and publisher and writes both in Polish and English. She edits the magazine *The Literary Memoir* and *Contemporary Writers of Poland*. Her publications include poems, short stories, and essays, and she has published an anthology *Flying Between Words, Contemporary Writers of Poland*. Her honors include the Gloria Artis medal for Merit to Culture by the Polish Ministry of Culture, the Cross of Freedom and Solidarity, and The Joseph Conrad Literary Prize (USA). Poems copyright © by Anna Maria Mickiewicz.

Stephen Paul Miller is the author of nine books of poems and two scholarly monographs, and has co-edited two additional scholarly volumes. His plays have been performed in New York and in San Francisco. He originated the Ear Inn Poetry Reading Series, and edited the *National Poetry Magazine of the Lower East Side*, the Poetry Mailing List, and *Critiphoria*. He is Professor of English and American Studies at St. John's University in New York City. "Beautiful Snacks" is in *Beautiful Snacks* (2022). "Tonight" was published in *Live Mag*. "Evensong," in a different version, appeared in the *St. Mark's Poetry Newsletter*. Poems copyright © by Stephen Paul Miller.

Wilda Morris, past President of the Illinois State Poetry Society, has published two books of poetry. She has won the 2019 Founders' Award from the National Federation of State Poetry Societies. "After I Argued with Francisco during Dinner…" was published in *The Ocotillo Review* and is copyright © by Wilda Morris.

Tim Murphy is the author of three chapbooks and his poems have appeared in many journals and magazines. Originally from Cork in Ireland, he lives in Madrid. "In a Mountain Dream" was published in his *The Cacti Do Not Move* and is copyright © by Tim Murphy.

David Nadeau lives in Quebec City, where he runs the publishing house La Vertèbre et le Rossignol, as well as the magazine of the same name. He is author of three collections and his works have appeared in many surrealist exhibitions and publications. "Dark Healer Dream" was published in *Peculiar Mormyrid* and is copyright © by David Nadeau.

KB Nelson is a Canadian writer whose poems have appeared in a variety of journals and anthologies and in one collection. She currently lives on the unceded territory of the Sechelt First Nation on British Columbia's Sunshine Coast. "Unspoken Words" appeared in *SurVision* and is copyright © by KB Nelson.

Kathryn Nocerino is author of three books of poetry, a Pushcart Prize nominee, and is widely anthologized in short fiction and poetry. Poem copyright © by Kathryn Nocerino.

Ciaran O'Driscoll lives in Limerick. A member of Aosdána, he has published eight books of poetry, a number of which were translated into other languages; a childhood memoir, *A Runner Among Falling Leaves* (2001); and a novel, *A Year's Midnight*. His awards include the James Joyce Prize and the Patrick and Katherine Kavanagh Fellowship in Poetry. His poem 'Please Hold' (featured in Forward's anthology *Poems of the Decade*) has become a set text for A Level English Literature. All five poems submitted have been published in *Angel Hour* (SurVision Books, 2021), and are copyright © by Ciaran O'Driscoll.

John Olson is the author of numerous books of prose poetry, essays, and fiction. He is also the author of five novels. In 2004, Olson received the annual Genius Award for Literature from Seattle's popular weekly *The Stranger*. Poems copyright © by John Olson.

Bart Plantenga has published poetry, novels, a short story collection, and books on yodeling. He's also a DJ and has produced the "Wreck This Mess" radio show in New York, Paris, and Amsterdam for many years. He lives in Amsterdam. Poem copyright © by Bart Plantenga.

Rochelle Potkar is a poet, editor, translator, fiction writer, and screenwriter. Her book of haibun, *Paper Asylum*, was shortlisted for the Rabindranath Tagore Literary Prize 2020. *Bombay Hangovers*, her collection of sixteen short stories, examines caste, class, and religion in Mumbai. Poem copyright © by Rochelle Potkar.

Orna Rav-Hon is a Hebrew Israeli poet who has published four books that make use of images and metaphors from the *Kabbalah*. She is recipient of the Tel Aviv Prize for Culture and Literature and the President Prize. She is a member of the Executive Committee of the Hebrew Writers Association in Israel. These poems were previously published in her book *Firebird* and are copyright © by Orna Rav-Hon.

Bronwyn Rodden is an Australian writer and artist. She was selected for the New Poets Program at Wollongong University, Australia, and was awarded an Emerging Writer Grant by the Australia Council for the Arts as well as a Fellowship to the Writers Cottage at Bundanon. She has published collections of short fiction and novels and is currently working on two collections of poetry. Poems copyright © by Bronwyn Rodden.

Rod Carlos Rodriguez has published three collections of poetry, including *Exploits of a Sun Poet*, which received the San Antonio Barnes and Noble/Bookstop Author of the Month Award and Best Book 2005 by the *San Antonio Current*. He is the founder and host of South Texas' longest running weekly open-mic poetry reading, the Sun Poet's Society Open-Mic Readings, and has been nominated for the San Antonio Poet

Lawrence R. Smith edited and published the now retired *Calibanonline* and its print parent, *Caliban*. He is the author of six volumes of poetry and translations. "Monkey in the Moonlight, with Birds" appeared in *Caliban* and "Second Sight" in *Calibanonline*. Poems copyright © by Lawrence R. Smith.

John Snelling won first prize in the City of Westminster Arts Council's poetry competition, and a Judge's Special Commendation in The Poetry Box competition for dark and horror poetry. He is one of the Keats House Poetry Ambassadors and regularly arranges and participates in poetry readings at Keats House in London. "Roads to Freedom" and "Fantasy" were published in *Siren Songs*; "Interim Police Report on Samuel Taylor Coleridge" was published in *Acumen:84*. Poems copyright © by John Snelling.

Sou Vai Keng, born in Macau in 1966, is a literary and visual artist. As a painter, Sou specializes in abstract ink painting. Recently, she has been exploring with color pencils the possibility of hiking with lines and colors on paper. Her literary work includes play scripts, novels, short stories, poetry, and poetry translations. Poems copyright © by Sou Vai Keng.

Ruth Stacey is a lecturer in creative writing at the University of Worcester. She has published six collections, including *Inheritance,* a duet with Katy Wareham Morris, which won the Best Collaborative Work in the 2018 Saboteur Awards. Poems copyright © Ruth Stacey.

Wally Swist has published more than forty-five books: collections of poetry, translations, volumes of haiku, children's books, nonfiction, belles lettres, audiobooks, and scholarly monographs, for which he has received many recognitions and awards. He is the subject of a biographical documentary film about his life. Poems copyright © by Wally Swist.

Jüri Talvet has published twenty books of poetry and essays in Estonian. His books have appeared in English, Spanish, French, Italian, Russian, Romanian, Serbian, Japanese, Catalan and Greek. He has been awarded the Estonian Annual Prize for Literature, the Juhan Liiv Prize for Poetry, the Ivar Ivask Memorial Prize, the Naji Naaman International Literature Honor Prize, and the Estonian National Science Prize for Lifework. Poems here are from *Yet, Love Illumine Us and Other Poems*, translated from the Estonian by Jüri Talvet and H. L. Hix, and are copyright © by Jüri Talvet and H. L. Hix.

Thomas Townsley's books include *Reading The Empty Page* and *Night Class For Insomniacs* by Black Rabbit Press, *Tangent of Ardency* by SurVision Books, and *Holding a Séance by Myself* by Standing Stone Books. In addition to writing,

Townsley plays blues harmonica and dabbles in painting. He teaches English and Creative Writing at Mohawk Valley Community College in Utica, NY.

John J. Trause, the Director of Oradell Public Library, is the author of seven collections, and his work appears internationally in many journals and anthologies, and as broadsides. He is a founder of the William Carlos Williams Poetry Cooperative in Rutherford, N. J. and former host and curator of its monthly reading series. His artwork has been widely exhibited. For the sake of art, Mr. Trause hung naked for one month in the summer of 2007 on the Art Wall of the Bowery Poetry Club. He is fond of cunning acrostics and color-coded chiasmus

Bjag Turing's race, gender, sexual orientation and national origin are indeterminate. This is their biography: Bjag Turing creates poetry. Poems copyright © by Bjag Turing.

Philip Venzke grew up on a dairy farm in Wisconsin. His most recent poems have appeared widely and he takes great pride in the fact that none of his poems have won any awards. "Odor of Sanctity" was published in *Survision* and "Dangerous Footprints" was published in *Opaque to Radiant*, both copyright © by Philip Venzke. Sarah Webb edited poetry for *Crosstimbers* at the University of Science and Arts of Oklahoma and presently co-edits the Zen magazine *Just This*. Her collection *Black* was named a finalist for the Oklahoma Book Award and for the Writers' League of Texas Book Award. Her *Red Riding Hood's Sister* was also short-listed for the Oklahoma Book Award. Poems copyright © by Sarah Webb.

Dorit Weisman lives in Jerusalem. She has received the EASAL (European Academy of Sciences, Arts and Letters), the International Poetry Prize Alfonso Gatto, theYehuda-Amichai Prize for Poetry, and the Prime Minister Prize for Israeli writers. She has published eleven volumes of poetry, two prose books, two translations, and edited three social protest anthologies. "Bolivar" was published in *Scrambled Eggs in Jerusalem* and is copyright © by Dorit Weisman.

Les Wicks has published in over 400 different magazines, anthologies and newspapers across thirty-two countries in fifteen languages. He runs Meuse Press, which focuses on poetry outreach projects like poetry on buses and poetry published on the surface of a river. His fourteenth book of poetry is *Belief*. "We Made it, It Made Us" was published in *Australian Poetry Journal*; "Perhaps the Adventure" was published in *Belief*; "Railway Town" was published in *Backstory*. Poems copyright © by Les Wicks.

Scott Wiggerman, a 2021 inductee into the Texas Institute of Letters, is the author of three books of poetry and the editor of several volumes, including *22 Poems and a*